WHAT IS CINEMA?

WHAT IS CINEMA?

by ANDRÉ BAZIN

essays selected and translated
by **HUGH GRAY**

UNIVERSITY OF CALIFORNIA PRESS

Berkeley   Los Angeles   London

UNIVERSITY OF CALIFORNIA PRESS
Berkeley and Los Angeles, California

UNIVERSITY OF CALIFORNIA PRESS, LTD.
London, England

ISBN: 0-520-00092-7

Library of Congress Catalog Card No.: 67–18899

17   18   19   20

FOREWORD

by Jean Renoir

IN THE DAYS when kings were kings, when they washed the feet of the poor and, by the simple act of passing by, healed those afflicted with scrofula, there were poets to confirm their belief in their greatness. Not infrequently the singer was greater than the object of his singing. This is where Bazin stands vis-à-vis the cinema. But that part of the story has to do only with what lies ahead. What is going on now is simply the assembling of materials. Civilization is but a sieve through the holes of which there passes the discard. The good remains. I am convinced that in Villon's day poets abounded on the banks of the Seine. Where are they now? Who were they? No one knows. But Villon is there still, large as life.

Our children and our grandchildren will have an invaluable source of help in sorting through the remains of the past. They will have Bazin alongside them. For that king of our time, the cinema, has likewise its poet. A modest fellow, sickly, slowly and prematurely dying, he it was who gave the patent of royalty to the cinema just as the poets of the past had crowned their kings. That king on whose brow he has placed a crown of glory is all the greater for having been stripped by him of the falsely glittering robes that hampered its progress. It is, thanks to him, a royal personage rendered healthy, cleansed of its parasites, fined down—a king of quality—that our grandchildren will delight to come upon. And in that same moment they will also discover its poet. They will discover André Bazin, discover too, as I have discovered, that only too often, the singer has once more risen above the object of his song.

There is no doubt about the influence that Bazin will have in the years to come. His writings will survive even if the cinema does not. Perhaps future generations will only know of its existence through his writings. Men will try to imagine a screen, with horses galloping across it, a close-up of a beautiful star, or the rolling eye of a dying hero, and each will interpret these things in his own way. But they will all agree on one thing, namely, the high quality of *What is Cinema?* This will be true even should these pages—saved from the wreckage—speak to us only of an art that is gone, just as archaeological remains bring to light the objects of cults that we are incapable any longer of imagining.

There is, then, no doubt as to Bazin's influence on the future. Let me say however that it is for his influence on his contemporaries that I hold him so deep in my affections. He made us feel that our trade was a noble one much in the same way that the saints of old persuaded the slave of the value of his humanity.

It is our good fortune to have Hugh Gray as the translator of these essays. It was a difficult task. Hugh Gray solved the problem by allowing himself to become immersed in Bazin—something that called for considerable strength of personality. Luckily alike for the translator, for the author, and for us, Bazin and Gray belong to the same spiritual family. Through the pages that follow they invite us, too, to become its adopted children.

CONTENTS

CONTENTS

INTRODUCTION

By Hugh Gray

IT IS NEARLY nine years since André Bazin died, but the critical insight that illuminates his writings has not grown dim with the years. It continues to shine forth in its very personal way, and the arguments through which he diffused it offer a brilliant example of a combination of the critical spirit and the spirit of synthesis, each operating with equal force. Bazin's thought, while rooted in a rich cultural tradition, produces conclusions that at times are forcefully expressed in terms drawn from contemporary science—an ambivalence which contributes markedly to his style and as markedly to the problems of a translator. Scattered among allusions drawn from literature, poetry, philosophy, and religion are analogies from chemistry, electricity, geology, psychology, and physics. Indeed, there are moments when one pictures Bazin as a poet in dungarees. Then again there are moments when one is aware of the teacher he was trained to be, was denied the opportunity to be (inside the classroom), yet has succeeded in being both in France and abroad. Those who, so to speak, had the good fortune to sit at his feet, tell us that what remains on paper is but a fragment of his wondrous discourse.

1

André Bazin was born on April 18, 1918, at Angers. He received his early schooling at La Rochelle, where he was taken at the age of five. Destined for the teaching profession, he entered training college first at La Rochelle and subsequently studied at Versailles. Then, in 1938, he transferred to the École Normale Supérieure at St. Cloud. He completed his studies there with a brilliant qualifying examination but, because of a stammer, was eventually refused a teaching post.

His intense interest in films seems to date from his early days in the army, to which he was called in 1939. Guy Leger, his then companion in arms, recounts that from the very outset Bazin tended to center his interest on speculative questions relating to film. "He was already attracted to the study of the true value of the cinematographic image as well as to the historical and social aspects of cinema. At that time, when the world seemed to be going to extremes in another direction, we turned to motion pictures as an escape from the 'phony war.' " What Guy Leger here says concerning their common interest is a foreshadowing of what was repeated constantly throughout the years by everyone who knew and shared his interest in the cinema. "What had been for me up to then only a pastime now began to appear, under the tutelage of André, a product of the age of the image, something that needed study if one was to savor its true flavor and understand its real significance; to make out its true language and to discover its objective laws."

Another friend, the critic P. A. Touchard, said of him early in their acquaintance that he found Bazin deeply impressive not only for his charm and his generosity of spirit but for his prodigious capacity for critical analysis as well as for an intense poetic sensibility. "No one," says Touchard, "had a greater command of words than this man who stammered when he spoke—and who had likewise a fantastic appetite for the consumption of scientific, philosophical, and abstract terms. Yet he was in no sense a pedant, remaining ever in command of the appropriate use of all these terms."

During the war he was a member of an organization—the Maison des Lettres—which was founded to take care of young students whose regular scholastic routine the war had disturbed. There he founded a ciné-club which developed out of meetings at which he defied the Nazi forces of occupation and the Vichy government by showing films they had banned for political reasons. His passion for the cinema, we are told and can readily believe, was part of his passion for culture and truth, allied to a moral authority which gave him the command over others that he exercised over himself—not only throughout a long inner spiritual conflict but also throughout a lifelong heroic struggle with the disease that was to take him off at the height of his intellectual powers. It has indeed been said that he was something of a mystic, although one would rather incline to think of him instead as a poet very much of his time. Always too there was in him that capacity characteristic of great teachers to bring out what was best in others, well described by Touchard as a "Socratic capacity to make those who talked to him seem intelligent to themselves." Indeed one might call him the Aristotle of the cinema and his writing its *Poetics*.

At the end of the occupation he was appointed film critic of *Le Parisien Liberé*. Thus began his formal life as a public critic and with it the development of a type of reviewing of films the like of which had not up to then existed. One of his singular achievements was to be able, without any concessions to popularizing, to make his insights understood on all levels. It was said of him at the time that in ten years he would become the outstanding French film critic. It took him less time than that. To us, his most commonly known association is with *Les Cahiers du Cinéma* which under his direction became one of the world's most distinguished film publications.

Meanwhile his other film activities multiplied, among them an appointment as director of cultural services at the Institut des Hautes Études Cinématographiques. He was thus appointed to a school at last. At a time when the word *filmology,* now well established, did not exist, "by his own efforts Bazin created," says Jean-Louis Tellenay, "a cinematographic culture." Nor can one adequately estimate the actual effect of his work on the cinema itself. "André staggered me," Tellenay continues, "at this time by his knowledge of a subject which one day, all unsuspected by us, would become a veritable discipline to be admitted into the halls of the Sorbonne."

Tellenay is here referring to the Institute of Filmology, as it came to be known, the philosophy of which was first set forth by Cohen-Séat in his *Essai sur les principes d'une philosophie du cinéma* (1958).

To those who hold that the intellect, as represented in the works of Bazin, divides man from his fellows and separates him off from the world, one need only offer the verdict of a man who knew Bazin intimately—Alexandre Astruc. "This theoretician, this intellectual, this idealist, this believer, was considerably closer to the realities of life and to his fellow man than those who reject the approach to life of a Bazin." François Truffaut, whom he befriended and whom he helped "probably more than anyone else," found that even to be scolded by Bazin was a delight, "such a heat did he generate in his rare moments of indignation. When it was over, one never said, 'how wrong I was,' only 'how right he is! how terrific!' "

Robert Bresson, as usual highly perceptive, points out a marked characteristic of Bazin's method. "He had a curious way of taking off from what was false to arrive ultimately at what was true." In a sense he was following in this, possibly quite deliberately, the old scholastic method: to state the thesis and to follow the statement with a denial before proceeding to the proof. However you see it, each essay is virtually a scientific demonstration, as Eric Rohmer points out in his assessment of the first volume of *Qu'est-ce que le cinéma?* "These pages, each relating to an individual case, are nevertheless part of the unfolding of a methodical plan which is now revealed to us. Nor is there the slightest doubt but that it was so conceived from the beginning, rather than being the outcome of a series of afterthoughts. While logic in his unfolding rather than chronology is his aim, it is strangely significant that the volume opens with an article on *The Ontology of the Photographic Image,* which is one of his earliest pieces. It is this scientific aspect of his work that I would like to dwell on without underestimating the art of it," Rohmer says. "Each essay and indeed the whole work itself fits perfectly into the pattern of a mathematical demonstration. Without any doubt, the whole body of Bazin's work is based on one central idea, an affirmation of the objectivity of the cinema in the same way as all geometry is centered on the properties of a straight line. Nor does he attempt to fit his basic principles at all costs into some alien system of aesthetics. They derive solely from his own thinking. The system followed by critics before him was, usually, to start with a definition of art and then to try and see how film fitted into it. Bazin rejects all the commonly accepted notions and proposes a radical change of perspective."

Many might expect that this "theoretician," this "intellectual" would be among those who deplore the passing of the silent film as the coming to an end of an art. Not so. For him, sound came not to destroy but to fulfill the testament of cinema. This is a position that follows directly from his central theme of the objectivity of cinema and leads him to reject, at least by implication, those who in the middle twenties were in search of pure cinema—or as Sadoul calls it, "the myth of pure cinema." Hence his preoccupation with adaptation as it relates both to theater and to the novel, and indeed to the relation between cinema and painting.

No one, to my knowledge, has challenged Bazin's stature as a critic but some other critics have had their moments of disagreement with him. Notable among these is Jean Mitry, another respected figure in the realm of film history and aesthetics, whose two-volume study *Ésthetique et psychologie du cinéma* has recently appeared. Although throughout this work he praises Bazin more often than he condemns him, he does in fact challenge—and by no means altogether unjustifiably, it would seem to me—the central concept of Bazin's critical structure, namely the objective reality of the filmic image, as well as Bazin's arguments on deep-focus photography. The reader will see how often this use of the camera is referred to, and in how many contexts, from a discussion of the films of Renoir to an examination of the true role of montage.

In "The Evolution of the Language of Cinema" Bazin speaks of the image as being evaluated not according to what it adds to reality but what it reveals of it. This Mitry challenges, refusing to accept the argument that because the camera automatically registers a given "reality" it gives us an objective and impartial image of that reality. What the camera reveals, Mitry argues, is not the reality in itself but a new appearance correlated to the world of things—what indeed one may call a camera-perception which, irrespective of the will of the cameraman, produces a certain "segregation of space," that is to say, a restructuring of the real so that it can no longer be considered "objective and immediate."

It is likewise on his theory of film objectivity that Bazin bases his refusal to agree that the essence of theater resides, as Henri Gouhier puts it, in the physical presence of the actor, thus setting it apart from cinema in one very basic respect. As a corollary of this famed argument, Bazin holds that the cinematic image is more than a reproduction, rather is it a thing in nature, a mold or masque. It is in this area that I myself find him difficult to follow. Here for once perhaps he goes beyond the realm of fact into the brilliantly created world of the "ben trovato."

Of his exuberant enthusiasm for the cinema, however, no better expression is to be found than his description of the film brought back from the Kon-Tiki expedition. The style of it is quintessential Bazin. But while there is the ubiquitous paradox, for once no scientific terms are pressed into service. One feels so clearly in reading it the vivid presence of the raft, the "flotsam" against which the fauna of the Pacific rub shoulders, their actions recorded in a film "snatched from the tempest"—a photographic record not so much

6

of things but of the danger which the camera shared—a film whose very faults are witness to its authenticity.

If I were asked to name the most perfectly wrought piece of film criticism that I have ever read I would unhesitatingly name the essay on the style of Robert Bresson. Furthermore, this essay contains what for me is an unforgettable summing up of the adaptation of a novel to the screen. Concerning the way Bresson handled *Jacques le fataliste,* the novel from which *Les Dames du Bois de Boulogne* was derived, Bazin writes: "The sound of a windshield wiper against a page of Diderot is all it took to turn it into Racinian dialogue." To this phrase I would apply the one Bazin used to describe his own delight in the work of Charlie Chaplin. In reading it one experiences "the delight of . . . recognizing perfection."

Today at last, due in no small part to André Bazin, the cinema is being widely recognized as a serious and important field of study. Too many for too long, notably in the United States, have preferred to think of it simply as an avenue of escape *par excellence* from a high-pressure life, for which we are ever seeking—a new world, as it were, to live in. But such so-called paths of escape, pleasant as they are to wander in, are in reality each but a cul-de-sac. The more we see the screen as a mirror rather than an escape hatch, the more we will be prepared for what is to come. Automation, we are told, will wipe the sweat from the brow and straighten the back of an Adam hitherto condemned to labor. Then will come the ultimate confrontation that man has so long avoided on the grounds that he must first live before he can philosophize. The cinema is capable, in the right hands, of playing an increasingly important role in this confrontation. For helping us to understand how or why this can be so, André Bazin may rightly be acclaimed a true visionary and guide. Supremely he is one of the few who have genuinely helped to answer the question first asked by Canudo, Delluc, and the other pioneers of film aesthetics and filmology—What is cinema?

Those of us who in his footsteps are likewise concerned to answer this question and who must therefore reach out, as he did, beyond the screen to the realms of history, philosophy, literature, psychology, sociology in search of the answer, and in the process add another dimension to the humanities, are particularly in the debt of this preceptor.

And now I have certain other debts to pay, first of all to Madame Janine Bazin who in every negotiation concerned with this undertaking has been graciousness itself. In addition I wish to acknowledge that without the generous help of Jean Renoir, of whose genius Bazin was an ardent and outspoken admirer, and of my colleagues Drs. Madeleine Korol and Gabriel Bonno, I would not have been able to render many difficult passages into English. I am grateful also to one of my students, Señor Markowitz of the Argentine, who assisted me in comparing my English with the Spanish translation. Finally, I am also deeply indebted to the special number of *Cahiers du Cinéma* dedicated to André Bazin for the facts and impressions there recorded by his friends.

THE ONTOLOGY
OF THE PHOTOGRAPHIC IMAGE

IF THE plastic arts were put under psychoanalysis, the practice of embalming the dead might turn out to be a fundamental factor in their creation. The process might reveal that at the origin of painting and sculpture there lies a mummy complex. The religion of ancient Egypt, aimed against death, saw survival as depending on the continued existence of the corporeal body. Thus, by providing a defense against the passage of time it satisfied a basic psychological need in man, for death is but the victory of time. To preserve, artificially, his bodily appearance is to snatch it from the flow of time, to stow it away neatly, so to speak, in the hold of life. It was natural, therefore, to keep up appearances in the face of the reality of death by preserving flesh and bone. The first Egyptian statue, then, was a mummy, tanned and petrified in sodium. But pyramids and labyrinthine corridors offered no certain guarantee against ultimate pillage.

Other forms of insurance were therefore sought. So, near the sarcophagus, alongside the corn that was to feed the dead, the Egyptians placed terra cotta statuettes, as substitute mummies which might replace the bodies if these were destroyed. It is this religious use, then, that lays bare the primordial function of statuary, namely, the preservation of life by a representation of life. Another manifestation of the same kind of thing is the arrow-pierced clay bear to be found in prehistoric caves, a magic identity-substitute for the living animal, that will ensure a successful hunt. The evolution, side by side, of art and civilization has relieved the plastic arts of their magic role. Louis XIV did not have himself embalmed. He was content to survive in his portrait by Le Brun. Civilization cannot, however, entirely cast out the bogy of time. It can only sublimate our concern with it to the level of rational thinking. No one believes any longer in the ontological identity of model and image, but all are agreed that the image helps us to remember the subject and to preserve him from a second spiritual death. Today the making of images no longer shares an anthropocentric, utilitarian purpose. It is no longer a question of survival after death, but of a larger concept, the creation of an ideal world in the likeness of the real, with its own temporal destiny. "How vain a thing is painting" if underneath our fond admiration for its works we do not discern man's primitive need to have the last word in the argument with death by means of the form that endures. If the history of the plastic arts is less a matter of their aesthetic than of their psychology then it will be seen to be essentially the story of resemblance, or, if you will, of realism.

Seen in this sociological perspective photography and cinema would provide a natural explanation for the great spiritual and technical crisis that overtook modern painting around the middle of the last century. André Malraux has described the cinema as the furthermost evolution to date of plastic realism, the beginnings of which were first manifest at the Renaissance and which found its completest expression in baroque painting.

It is true that painting, the world over, has struck a varied balance between the symbolic and realism. However, in the fifteenth century Western painting began to turn from its age-old concern with spiritual realities expressed in the form proper to it, towards an effort to combine this spiritual expression with as complete an imitation as possible of the outside world.

The decisive moment undoubtedly came with the discovery of the first scientific and already, in a sense, mechanical system of reproduction, namely, perspective: the camera obscura of Da Vinci foreshadowed the camera of Niepce. The artist was now in a position to create the illusion of three-dimensional space within which things appeared to exist as our eyes in reality see them.

Thenceforth painting was torn between two ambitions: one, primarily aesthetic, namely the expression of spiritual reality wherein the symbol transcended its model; the other, purely psychological, namely the duplication of the world outside. The satisfaction of this appetite for illusion merely served to increase it till, bit by bit, it consumed the plastic arts. However, since perspective had only solved the problem of form and not of movement, realism was forced to continue the search for some way of giving dramatic expression to the moment, a kind of psychic fourth dimension that could suggest life in the tortured immobility of baroque art.*

The great artists, of course, have always been able to combine the two tendencies. They have allotted to each its proper place in the hierarchy of things, holding reality at their command and molding it at will into the fabric of their art. Nevertheless, the fact remains that we are faced with two essentially different phenomena and these any objective critic must view separately if he is to understand the evolution of the pictorial. The need for illusion has not ceased to trouble the heart of painting since the sixteenth century. It is a purely mental need, of itself nonaesthetic, the origins of which must be sought in the proclivity of the mind towards magic. However, it is a need the pull of which has been strong enough to have seriously upset the equilibrium of the plastic arts.

---

* It would be interesting from this point of view to study, in the illustrated magazines of 1890–1910, the rivalry between photographic reporting and the use of drawings. The latter, in particular, satisfied the baroque need for the dramatic. A feeling for the photographic document developed only gradually.

The quarrel over realism in art stems from a misunderstanding, from a confusion between the aesthetic and the psychological; between true realism, the need that is to give significant expression to the world both concretely and its essence, and the pseudorealism of a deception aimed at fooling the eye (or for that matter the mind); a pseudorealism content in other words with illusory appearances.* That is why medieval art never passed through this crisis; simultaneously vividly realistic and highly spiritual, it knew nothing of the drama that came to light as a consequence of technical developments. Perspective was the original sin of Western painting.

It was redeemed from sin by Niepce and Lumière. In achieving the aims of baroque art, photography has freed the plastic arts from their obsession with likeness. Painting was forced, as it turned out, to offer us illusion and this illusion was reckoned sufficient unto art. Photography and the cinema on the other hand are discoveries that satisfy, once and for all and in its very essence, our obsession with realism.

No matter how skillful the painter, his work was always in fee to an inescapable subjectivity. The fact that a human hand intervened cast a shadow of doubt over the image. Again, the essential factor in the transition from the baroque to photography is not the perfecting of a physical process (photography will long remain the inferior of painting in the reproduction of color); rather does it lie in a psychological fact, to wit, in completely satisfying our appetite for illusion by a mechanical reproduction in the making of which man plays no part. The solution is not to be found in the result achieved but in the way of achieving it.†

---

* Perhaps the Communists, before they attach too much importance to expressionist realism, should stop talking about it in a way more suitable to the eighteenth century, before there were such things as photography or cinema. Maybe it does not really matter if Russian painting is second-rate provided Russia gives us first-rate cinema. Eisenstein is her Tintoretto.

† There is room, nevertheless, for a study of the psychology of the lesser plastic arts, the molding of death masks for example, which likewise involves a certain automatic process. One might consider photography in this sense as a molding, the taking of an impression, by the manipulation of light.

This is why the conflict between style and likeness is a relatively modern phenomenon of which there is no trace before the invention of the sensitized plate. Clearly the fascinating objectivity of Chardin is in no sense that of the photographer. The nineteenth century saw the real beginnings of the crisis of realism of which Picasso is now the mythical central figure and which put to the test at one and the same time the conditions determining the formal existence of the plastic arts and their sociological roots. Freed from the "resemblance complex," the modern painter abandons it to the masses who, henceforth, identify resemblance on the one hand with photography and on the other with the kind of painting which is related to photography.

Originality in photography as distinct from originality in painting lies in the essentially objective character of photography. [Bazin here makes a point of the fact that the lens, the basis of photography, is in French called the "objectif," a nuance that is lost in English.—Tr.] For the first time, between the originating object and its reproduction there intervenes only the instrumentality of a nonliving agent. For the first time an image of the world is formed automatically, without the creative intervention of man. The personality of the photographer enters into the proceedings only in his selection of the object to be photographed and by way of the purpose he has in mind. Although the final result may reflect something of his personality, this does not play the same role as is played by that of the painter. All the arts are based on the presence of man, only photography derives an advantage from his absence. Photography affects us like a phenomenon in nature, like a flower or a snowflake whose vegetable or earthly origins are an inseparable part of their beauty.

This production by automatic means has radically affected our psychology of the image. The objective nature of photography confers on it a quality of credibility absent from all other picture-making. In spite of any objections our critical spirit may offer, we are forced to accept as real the existence of the object reproduced,

13

actually *re*-presented, set before us, that is to say, in time and space. Photography enjoys a certain advantage in virtue of this transference of reality from the thing to its reproduction.*

A very faithful drawing may actually tell us more about the model but despite the promptings of our critical intelligence it will never have the irrational power of the photograph to bear away our faith.

Besides, painting is, after all, an inferior way of making likenesses, an *ersatz* of the processes of reproduction. Only a photographic lens can give us the kind of image of the object that is capable of satisfying the deep need man has to substitute for it something more than a mere approximation, a kind of decal or transfer. The photographic image is the object itself, the object freed from the conditions of time and space that govern it. No matter how fuzzy, distorted, or discolored, no matter how lacking in documentary value the image may be, it shares, by virtue of the very process of its becoming, the being of the model of which it is the reproduction; it *is* the model.

Hence the charm of family albums. Those grey or sepia shadows, phantomlike and almost undecipherable, are no longer traditional family portraits but rather the disturbing presence of lives halted at a set moment in their duration, freed from their destiny; not, however, by the prestige of art but by the power of an impassive mechanical process: for photography does not create eternity, as art does, it embalms time, rescuing it simply from its proper corruption.

Viewed in this perspective, the cinema is objectivity in time. The film is no longer content to preserve the object, enshrouded as it were in an instant, as the bodies of insects are preserved intact, out of the distant past, in amber. The film delivers baroque art from

---

* Here one should really examine the psychology of relics and souvenirs which likewise enjoy the advantages of a transfer of reality stemming from the "mummy-complex." Let us merely note in passing that the Holy Shroud of Turin combines the features alike of relic and photograph.

its convulsive catalepsy. Now, for the first time, the image of things is likewise the image of their duration, change mummified as it were. Those categories of *resemblance* which determine the species *photographic* image likewise, then, determine the character of its aesthetic as distinct from that of painting.*

The aesthetic qualities of photography are to be sought in its power to lay bare the realities. It is not for me to separate off, in the complex fabric of the objective world, here a reflection on a damp sidewalk, there the gesture of a child. Only the impassive lens, stripping its object of all those ways of seeing it, those piled-up preconceptions, that spiritual dust and grime with which my eyes have covered it, is able to present it in all its virginal purity to my attention and consequently to my love. By the power of photography, the natural image of a world that we neither know nor can see, nature at last does more than imitate art: she imitates the artist.

Photography can even surpass art in creative power. The aesthetic world of the painter is of a different kind from that of the world about him. Its boundaries enclose a substantially and essentially different microcosm. The photograph as such and the object in itself share a common being, after the fashion of a fingerprint. Wherefore, photography actually contributes something to the order of natural creation instead of providing a substitute for it. The surrealists had an inkling of this when they looked to the photographic plate to provide them with their monstrosities and for this reason: the surrealist does not consider his aesthetic purpose and the mechanical effect of the image on our imaginations as things apart. For him, the logical distinction between what is imaginary and what is real tends to disappear. Every image is to be

---

* I use the term *category* here in the sense attached to it by M. Gouhier in his book on the theater in which he distinguishes between the dramatic and the aesthetic categories. Just as dramatic tension has no artistic value, the perfection of a reproduction is not to be identified with beauty. It constitutes rather the prime matter, so to speak, on which the artistic fact is recorded.

seen as an object and every object as an image. Hence photography ranks high in the order of surrealist creativity because it produces an image that is a reality of nature, namely, an hallucination that is also a fact. The fact that surrealist painting combines tricks of visual deception with meticulous attention to detail substantiates this.

So, photography is clearly the most important event in the history of plastic arts. Simultaneously a liberation and a fulfillment, it has freed Western painting, once and for all, from its obsession with realism and allowed it to recover its aesthetic autonomy. Impressionist realism, offering science as an alibi, is at the opposite extreme from eye-deceiving trickery. Only when form ceases to have any imitative value can it be swallowed up in color. So, when form, in the person of Cézanne, once more regains possession of the canvas there is no longer any question of the illusions of the geometry of perspective. The painting, being confronted in the mechanically produced image with a competitor able to reach out beyond baroque resemblance to the very identity of the model, was compelled into the category of object. Henceforth Pascal's condemnation of painting is itself rendered vain since the photograph allows us on the one hand to admire in reproduction something that our eyes alone could not have taught us to love, and on the other, to admire the painting as a thing in itself whose relation to something in nature has ceased to be the justification for its existence.

On the other hand, of course, cinema is also a language.

THE MYTH OF TOTAL CINEMA

PARADOXICALLY enough, the impression left on the reader by Georges Sadoul's admirable book on the origins of the cinema is of a reversal, in spite of the author's Marxist views, of the relations between an economic and technical evolution and the imagination of those carrying on the search. The way things happened seems to call for a reversal of the historical order of causality, which goes from the economic infrastructure to the ideological superstructure, and for us to consider the basic technical discoveries as fortunate accidents but essentially second in importance to the preconceived ideas of the inventors. The cinema is an idealistic phenomenon. The concept men had of it existed so to speak fully armed in their minds, as if in some platonic heaven, and what strikes us most of all is the obstinate resistance of matter to ideas rather than of any help offered by techniques to the imagination of the researchers.

Furthermore, the cinema owes virtually nothing to the scientific spirit. Its begetters are in no sense savants, except for Marey, but it is significant that he was only interested in analyzing movement and not in reconstructing it. Even Edison is basically only a do-it-yourself man of genius, a giant of the *concours Lépine*. Niepce, Muybridge, Leroy, Joly, Demeny, even Louis Lumière himself, are all monomaniacs, men driven by an impulse, do-it-yourself men or

17

at best ingenious industrialists. As for the wonderful, the sublime E. Reynaud, who can deny that his animated drawings are the result of an unremitting pursuit of an *idée fixe?* Any account of the cinema that was drawn merely from the technical inventions that made it possible would be a poor one indeed. On the contrary, an approximate and complicated visualization of an idea invariably precedes the industrial discovery which alone can open the way to its practical use. Thus if it is evident to us today that the cinema even at its most elementary stage needed a transparent, flexible, and resistant base and a dry sensitive emulsion capable of receiving an image instantly—everything else being a matter of setting in order a mechanism far less complicated than an eighteenth-century clock—it is clear that all the definitive stages of the invention of the cinema had been reached before the requisite conditions had been fulfilled. In 1877 and 1880, Muybridge, thanks to the imaginative generosity of a horse-lover, managed to construct a large complex device which enabled him to make from the image of a galloping horse the first series of cinematographic pictures. However to get this result he had to be satisfied with wet collodion on a glass plate, that is to say, with just one of the three necessary elements— namely instantaneity, dry emulsion, flexible base. After the discovery of gelatino-bromide of silver but before the appearance on the market of the first celluloid reels, Marey had made a genuine camera which used glass plates. Even after the appearance of celluloid strips Lumière tried to use paper film.

Once more let us consider here only the final and complete form of the photographic cinema. The synthesis of simple movements studied scientifically by Plateau had no need to wait upon the industrial and economic developments of the nineteenth century. As Sadoul correctly points out, nothing had stood in the way, from antiquity, of the manufacture of a phenakistoscope or a zootrope. It is true that here the labors of that genuine savant Plateau were at the origin of the many inventions that made the popular use of his discovery possible. But while, with the photographic cinema, we have cause for some astonishment that the discovery somehow precedes the technical conditions necessary to its existence, we must here explain, on the other hand, how it was that the invention took so long to emerge, since all the prerequisites had been assembled and the persistence of the image on the retina had been known for a long time. It might be of some use to point out that although the two were not necessarily connected scientifically, the efforts of Plateau are pretty well contemporary with those of Nicéphore Niepce, as if the attention of researchers had waited to concern itself with synthesizing movement until chemistry quite independently of optics had become concerned, on its part, with the automatic fixing of the image.*

I emphasize the fact that this historical coincidence can apparently in no way be explained on grounds of scientific, economic, or industrial evolution. The photographic cinema could just as well have grafted itself onto a phenakistoscope foreseen as long ago as the sixteenth century. The delay in the invention of the latter is as disturbing a phenomenon as the existence of the precursors of the former.

But if we examine their work more closely, the direction of their research is manifest in the instruments themselves, and, even more undeniably, in their writings and commentaries we see that these precursors were indeed more like prophets. Hurrying past the vari-

* The frescoes or bas-reliefs of Egypt indicate a desire to analyze rather than to synthesize movement. As for the automatons of the eighteenth century their relation to cinema is like the relation of painting to photography. Whatever the truth of the matter and even if the automatons from the time of Descartes and Pascal on foreshadowed the machines of the nineteenth century, it is no different from the way that *trompe-l'oeil* in painting attested to a chronic taste for likeness. But the technique of *trompe-l'oeil* did nothing to advance optics and the chemistry of photography; it confined itself, if I can use the expression, to "playing the monkey" to them by anticipation.

Besides, just as the word indicates, the aesthetic of *trompe-l'oeil* in the eighteenth century resided more in illusion than in realism, that is to say, in a lie rather than the truth. A statue painted on a wall should look as if it were standing on a pedestal in space. To some extent, this is what the early cinema was aiming at, but this operation of cheating quickly gave way to an ontogenetic realism.

ous stopping places, the very first of which materially speaking should have halted them, it was at the very height and summit that most of them were aiming. In their imaginations they saw the cinema as a total and complete representation of reality; they saw in a trice the reconstruction of a perfect illusion of the outside world in sound, color, and relief.

As for the latter, the film historian P. Potoniée has even felt justified in maintaining that it was not the discovery of photography but of stereoscopy, which came onto the market just slightly before the first attempts at animated photography in 1851, that opened the eyes of the researchers. Seeing people immobile in space, the photographers realized that what they needed was movement if their photographs were to become a picture of life and a faithful copy of nature. In any case, there was not a single inventor who did not try to combine sound and relief with animation of the image—whether it be Edison with his kinetoscope made to be attached to a phonograph, or Demenay and his talking portraits, or even Nadar who shortly before producing the first photographic interview, on Chevreul, had written, "My dream is to see the photograph register the bodily movements and the facial expressions of a speaker while the phonograph is recording his speech" (February, 1887). If color had not yet appeared it was because the first experiments with the three-color process were slower in coming. But E. Reynaud had been painting his little figurines for some time and the first films of Méliès are colored by stencilling. There are numberless writings, all of them more or less wildly enthusiastic, in which inventors conjure up nothing less than a total cinema that is to provide that complete illusion of life which is still a long way away. Many are familiar with that passage from *L'Ève Future* in which Villiers de l'Isle-Adam, two years before Edison had begun his researches on animated photography, puts into the inventor's mouth the following description of a fantastic achievement: ". . . the vision, its transparent flesh miraculously photographed in color and wearing a spangled costume, danced a

20

kind of popular Mexican dance. Her movements had the flow of life itself, thanks to the process of successive photography which can retain six minutes of movement on microscopic glass, which is subsequently reflected by means of a powerful lampascope. Suddenly was heard a flat and unnatural voice, dull-sounding and harsh. The dancer was singing the *alza* and the *olé* that went with her *fandango*."

The guiding myth, then, inspiring the invention of cinema, is the accomplishment of that which dominated in a more or less vague fashion all the techniques of the mechanical reproduction of reality in the nineteenth century, from photography to the phonograph, namely an integral realism, a recreation of the world in its own image, an image unburdened by the freedom of interpretation of the artist or the irreversibility of time. If cinema in its cradle lacked all the attributes of the cinema to come, it was with reluctance and because its fairy guardians were unable to provide them however much they would have liked to.

If the origins of an art reveal something of its nature, then one may legitimately consider the silent and the sound film as stages of a technical development that little by little made a reality out of the original "myth." It is understandable from this point of view that it would be absurd to take the silent film as a state of primal perfection which has gradually been forsaken by the realism of sound and color. The primacy of the image is both historically and technically accidental. The nostalgia that some still feel for the silent screen does not go far enough back into the childhood of the seventh art. The real primitives of the cinema, existing only in the imaginations of a few men of the nineteenth century, are in complete imitation of nature. Every new development added to the cinema must, paradoxically, take it nearer and nearer to its origins. In short, cinema has not yet been invented!

It would be a reversal then of the concrete order of causality, at least psychologically, to place the scientific discoveries or the industrial techniques that have loomed so large in its development at the source of the cinema's invention. Those who had the least confidence in the future of the cinema were precisely the two industrialists Edison and Lumière. Edison was satisfied with just his kinetoscope and if Lumière judiciously refused to sell his patent to Méliès it was undoubtedly because he hoped to make a large profit out of it for himself, but only as a plaything of which the public would soon tire. As for the real savants such as Marey, they were only of indirect assistance to the cinema. They had a specific purpose in mind and were satisfied when they had accomplished it. The fanatics, the madmen, the disinterested pioneers, capable, as was Berard Palissy, of burning their furniture for a few seconds of shaky images, are neither industrialists nor savants, just men obsessed by their own imaginings. The cinema was born from the converging of these various obsessions, that is to say, out of a myth, the myth of total cinema. This likewise adequately explains the delay of Plateau in applying the optical principle of the persistence of the image on the retina, as also the continuous progress of the syntheses of movement as compared with the state of photographic techniques. The fact is that each alike was dominated by the imagination of the century. Undoubtedly there are other examples in the history of techniques and inventions of the convergence of research, but one must distinguish between those which come as a result precisely of scientific evolution and industrial or military requirements and those which quite clearly precede them. Thus, the myth of Icarus had to wait on the internal combustion engine before descending from the platonic heavens. But it had dwelt in the soul of everyman since he first thought about birds. To some extent, one could say the same thing about the myth of cinema, but its forerunners prior to the nineteenth century have only a remote connection with the myth which we share today and which has prompted the appearance of the mechanical arts that characterize today's world.

THE EVOLUTION
OF THE LANGUAGE OF CINEMA

BY 1928 the silent film had reached its artistic peak. The despair of its elite as they witnessed the dismantling of this ideal city, while it may not have been justified, is at least understandable. As they followed their chosen aesthetic path it seemed to them that the cinema had developed into an art most perfectly accommodated to the "exquisite embarrassment" of silence and that the realism that sound would bring could only mean a surrender to chaos.

In point of fact, now that sound has given proof that it came not to destroy but to fulfill the Old Testament of the cinema, we may most properly ask if the technical revolution created by the sound track was in any sense an aesthetic revolution. In other words, did the years from 1928 to 1930 actually witness the birth of a new cinema? Certainly, as regards editing, history does not actually show as wide a breach as might be expected between the silent and the sound film. On the contrary there is discernible evidence of a close relationship between certain directors of 1925 and 1935 and especially of the 1940's through the 1950's. Compare for example Erich von Stroheim and Jean Renoir or Orson Welles, or again Carl Theodore Dreyer and Robert Bresson. These more or less clear-cut affinities demonstrate first of all that the gap separating the 1920's and the 1930's can be bridged, and secondly that certain cinematic values actually carry over from the silent to the sound film and, above all, that it is less a matter of setting silence over against sound than of contrasting certain families of styles, certain basically different concepts of cinematographic expression.

Aware as I am that the limitations imposed on this study restrict me to a simplified and to that extent enfeebled presentation of my argument, and holding it to be less an objective statement than a working hypothesis, I will distinguish, in the cinema between 1920 and 1940, between two broad and opposing trends: those directors who put their faith in the image and those who put their faith in reality. By "image" I here mean, very broadly speaking, everything that the representation on the screen adds to the object there represented. This is a complex inheritance but it can be reduced essentially to two categories: those that relate to the plastics of the image and those that relate to the resources of montage, which, after all, is simply the ordering of images in time.

Under the heading "plastics" must be included the style of the sets, of the make-up, and, up to a point, even of the performance, to which we naturally add the lighting and, finally, the framing of the shot which gives us its composition. As regards montage, derived initially as we all know from the masterpieces of Griffith, we have the statement of Malraux in his *Psychologie du cinéma* that it was montage that gave birth to film as an art, setting it apart from mere animated photography, in short, creating a language.

The use of montage can be "invisible" and this was generally the case in the prewar classics of the American screen. Scenes were broken down just for one purpose, namely, to analyze an episode according to the material or dramatic logic of the scene. It is this logic which conceals the fact of the analysis, the mind of the spectator quite naturally accepting the viewpoints of the director which are justified by the geography of the action or the shifting emphasis of dramatic interest.

But the neutral quality of this "invisible" editing fails to make use of the full potential of montage. On the other hand these potentialities are clearly evident from the three processes generally known as parallel montage, accelerated montage, montage by attraction. In creating parallel montage, Griffith succeeded in conveying a sense of the simultaneity of two actions taking place at a geographical distance by means of alternating shots from each. In *La Roue* Abel Gance created the illusion of the steadily increasing speed of a locomotive without actually using any images of speed (indeed the wheel could have been turning on one spot) simply by a multiplicity of shots of ever-decreasing length.

Finally there is "montage by attraction," the creation of S. M. Eisenstein, and not so easily described as the others, but which may be roughly defined as the reenforcing of the meaning of one image by association with another image not necessarily part of the same episode—for example the fireworks display in *The General Line* following the image of the bull. In this extreme form, montage by attraction was rarely used even by its creator but one may consider as very near to it in principle the more commonly used ellipsis, comparison, or metaphor, examples of which are the throwing of stockings onto a chair at the foot of a bed, or the milk overflowing in H. G. Clouzot's *Quai des orfèvres*. There are of course a variety of possible combinations of these three processes.

Whatever these may be, one can say that they share that trait in common which constitutes the very definition of montage, namely, the creation of a sense or meaning not objectively contained in the images themselves but derived exclusively from their juxtaposition. The well-known experiment of Kuleshov with the shot of Mozhukhin in which a smile was seen to change its significance according to the image that preceded it, sums up perfectly the properties of montage.

Montage as used by Kuleshov, Eisenstein, or Gance did not show us the event; it alluded to it. Undoubtedly they derived at least the greater part of the constituent elements from the reality they were describing but the final significance of the film was found to reside in the ordering of these elements much more than in their objective content. The substance of the narrative, whatever the realism of the individual image, is born essentially from these relationships—Mozhukhin plus dead child equal pity—that is to say an abstract result, none of the concrete elements of which are to be found in the premises; maidens plus appletrees in bloom equal hope. The combinations are infinite. But the only thing they have in common is the fact that they suggest an idea by means of a metaphor or by an association of ideas. Thus between the scenario properly so-called, the ultimate object of the recital, and the image pure and simple, there is a relay station, a sort of aesthetic "transformer." The meaning is not in the image, it is in the shadow of the image projected by montage onto the field of consciousness of the spectator.

Let us sum up. Through the contents of the image and the resources of montage, the cinema has at its disposal a whole arsenal of means whereby to impose its interpretation of an event on the spectator. By the end of the silent film we can consider this arsenal to have been full. On the one side the Soviet cinema carried to its ultimate consequences the theory and practice of montage while the German school did every kind of violence to the plastics of the image by way of sets and lighting. Other cinemas count too besides the Russian and German, but whether in France or Sweden or the United States, it does not appear that the language of cinema was at a loss for ways of saying what it wanted to say.

If the art of cinema consists in everything that plastics and montage can add to a given reality, the silent film was an art on its own. Sound could only play at best a subordinate and supplementary role: a counterpoint to the visual image. But this possible enhancement—at best only a minor one—is likely not to weigh much in comparison with the additional bargain-rate reality introduced at the same time by sound.

Thus far we have put forward the view that expressionism of montage and image constitute the essence of cinema. And it is precisely on this generally accepted notion that directors from silent days, such as Erich von Stroheim, F. W. Murnau, and Robert Flaherty, have by implication cast a doubt. In their films, montage plays no part, unless it be the negative one of inevitable elimination where reality superabounds. The camera cannot see everything at once but it makes sure not to lose any part of what it chooses to see. What matters to Flaherty, confronted with Nanook hunting the seal, is the relation between Nanook and the animal; the actual length of the waiting period. Montage could suggest the time involved. Flaherty however confines himself to showing the actual waiting period; the length of the hunt is the very substance of the image, its true object. Thus in the film this episode requires one set-up. Will anyone deny that it is thereby much more moving than a montage by attraction?

Murnau is interested not so much in time as in the reality of dramatic space. Montage plays no more of a decisive part in *Nosferatu* than in *Sunrise*. One might be inclined to think that the plastics of his image are expressionistic. But this would be a superficial view. The composition of his image is in no sense pictorial. It adds nothing to the reality, it does not deform it, it forces it to reveal its structural depth, to bring out the preexisting relations which become constitutive of the drama. For example, in *Tabu,* the arrival of a ship from left screen gives an immediate sense of destiny at work so that Murnau has no need to cheat in any way on the uncompromising realism of a film whose settings are completely natural.

But it is most of all Stroheim who rejects photographic expressionism and the tricks of montage. In his films reality lays itself bare like a suspect confessing under the relentless examination of the commissioner of police. He has one simple rule for direction. Take a close look at the world, keep on doing so, and in the end it will lay bare for you all its cruelty and its ugliness. One could easily imagine as a matter of fact a film by Stroheim composed of a single shot as long-lasting and as close-up as you like. These three directors do not exhaust the possibilities. We would undoubtedly find scattered among the works of others elements of nonexpressionistic cinema in which montage plays no part—even including Griffith.

But these examples suffice to reveal, at the very heart of the silent film, a cinematographic art the very opposite of that which has been identified as *"cinéma par excellence,"* a language the semantic and syntactical unit of which is in no sense the Shot; in which the image is evaluated not according to what it adds to reality but what it reveals of it. In the latter art the silence of the screen was a drawback, that is to say, it deprived reality of one of its elements. *Greed,* like Dreyer's *Jeanne d'Arc,* is already virtually a talking film. The moment that you cease to maintain that montage and the plastic composition of the image are the very essence of the language of cinema, sound is no longer the aesthetic crevasse dividing two radically different aspects of the seventh art. The cinema that is believed to have died of the soundtrack is in no sense *"the* cinema." The real dividing line is elsewhere. It was operative in the past and continues to be through thirty-five years of the history of the language of the film.

Having challenged the aesthetic unity of the silent film and divided it off into two opposing tendencies, now let us take a look at the history of the last twenty years.

From 1930 to 1940 there seems to have grown up in the world, originating largely in the United States, a common form of cinematic language. It was the triumph in Hollywood, during that time, of five or six major kinds of film that gave it its overwhelming superiority: (1) American comedy (*Mr. Smith Goes to Washington,* 1936); (2) The burlesque film (The Marx Brothers); (3) The dance and vaudeville film (Fred Astaire and Ginger Rogers and the Ziegfield Follies); (4) The crime and gangster film (*Scarface, I Am a Fugitive from a Chain Gang, The Informer*); (5) Psychological and social dramas (*Back Street, Jezebel*); (6) Horror or fantasy films (*Dr. Jekyll and Mr. Hyde, The Invisible Man, Frankenstein*); (7) The western (*Stagecoach,* 1939). During that time the French cinema undoubtedly ranked next. Its superiority was gradually manifested by way of a trend towards what might be roughly called stark somber realism, or poetic realism, in which four names stand out: Jacques Feyder, Jean Renoir, Marcel Carné, and Julien Duvivier. My intention not being to draw up a list of prize-winners, there is little use in dwelling on the Soviet, British, German, or Italian films for which these years were less significant than the ten that were to follow. In any case, American and French production sufficiently clearly indicate that the sound film, prior to World War II, had reached a well-balanced stage of maturity.

First as to content. Major varieties with clearly defined rules capable of pleasing a worldwide public, as well as a cultured elite, provided it was not inherently hostile to the cinema.

Secondly as to form: well-defined styles of photography and editing perfectly adapted to their subject matter; a complete harmony of image and sound. In seeing again today such films as *Jezebel* by William Wyler, *Stagecoach* by John Ford, or *Le Jour se lève* by Marcel Carné, one has the feeling that in them an art has found its perfect balance, its ideal form of expression, and reciprocally one admires them for dramatic and moral themes to which the cinema, while it may not have created them, has given a grandeur, an artistic effectiveness, that they would not otherwise have had. In short, here are all the characteristics of the ripeness of a classical art.

I am quite aware that one can justifiably argue that the originality of the postwar cinema as compared with that of 1938 derives from the growth of certain national schools, in particular the dazzling display of the Italian cinema and of a native English cinema freed from the influence of Hollywood. From this one might conclude that the really important phenomenon of the years 1940–1950 is the introduction of new blood, of hitherto unexplored themes. That is to say, the real revolution took place more on the level of subject matter than of style. Is not neorealism primarily a kind of humanism and only secondarily a style of film-making? Then as to the style itself, is it not essentially a form of self-effacement before reality?

29

Our intention is certainly not to preach the glory of form over content. Art for art's sake is just as heretical in cinema as elsewhere, probably more so. On the other hand, a new subject matter demands new form, and as good a way as any towards understanding what a film is trying to say to us is to know how it is saying it.

Thus by 1938 or 1939 the talking film, particularly in France and in the United States, had reached a level of classical perfection as a result, on the one hand, of the maturing of different kinds of drama developed in part over the past ten years and in part inherited from the silent film, and, on the other, of the stabilization of technical progress. The 1930's were the years, at once, of sound and of panchromatic film. Undoubtedly studio equipment had continued to improve but only in matters of detail, none of them opening up new, radical possibilities for direction. The only changes in this situation since 1940 have been in photography, thanks to the increased sensitivity of the film stock. Panchromatic stock turned visual values upside down, ultrasensitive emulsions have made a modification in their structure possible. Free to shoot in the studio with a much smaller aperture, the operator could, when necessary, eliminate the soft-focus background once considered essential. Still there are a number of examples of the prior use of deep focus, for example in the work of Jean Renoir. This had always been possible on exteriors, and given a measure of skill, even in the studios. Anyone could do it who really wanted to. So that it is less a question basically of a technical problem, the solution of which has admittedly been made easier, than of a search after a style—a point to which we will come back. In short, with panchromatic stock in common use, with an understanding of the potentials of the microphone, and with the crane as standard studio equipment, one can really say that since 1930 all the technical requirements for the art of cinema have been available.

Since the determining technical factors were practically eliminated, we must look elsewhere for the signs and principles of the evolution of film language, that is to say by challenging the subject matter and as a consequence the styles necessary for its expression.

By 1939 the cinema had arrived at what geographers call the equilibrium-profile of a river. By this is meant that ideal mathematical curve which results from the requisite amount of erosion. Having reached this equilibrium-profile, the river flows effortlessly from its source to its mouth without further deepening of its bed. But if any geological movement occurs which raises the erosion level and modifies the height of the source, the water sets to work again, seeps into the surrounding land, goes deeper, burrowing and digging. Sometimes when it is a chalk bed, a new pattern is dug across the plain, almost invisible but found to be complex and winding, if one follows the flow of the water.

The Evolution of Editing since the Advent of Sound

In 1938 there was an almost universal standard pattern of editing. If, somewhat conventionally, we call the kind of silent films based on the plastics of the image and the artifices of montage, "expressionist" or "symbolistic," we can describe the new form of storytelling "analytic" and "dramatic." Let us suppose, by way of reviewing one of the elements of the experiment of Kuleshov, that we have a table covered with food and a hungry tramp. One can imagine that in 1936 it would have been edited as follows:

(1) Full shot of the actor and the table.
(2) Camera moves forward into a close-up of a face expressing a mixture of amazement and longing.
(3) Series of close-ups of food.
(4) Back to full shot of person who starts slowly towards the camera.
(5) Camera pulls slowly back to a three-quarter shot of the actor seizing a chicken wing.

Whatever variants one could think of for this scene, they would all have certain points in common:

(1) The verisimilitude of space in which the position of the

31

           actor is always determined, even when a close-up eliminates the decor.

    (2) The purpose and the effects of the cutting are exclusively dramatic or psychological.

In other words, if the scene were played on a stage and seen from a seat in the orchestra, it would have the same meaning, the episode would continue to exist objectively. The changes of point of view provided by the camera would add nothing. They would present the reality a little more forcefully, first by allowing a better view and then by putting the emphasis where it belongs.

It is true that the stage director like the film director has at his disposal a margin within which he is free to vary the interpretation of the action but it is only a margin and allows for no modification of the inner logic of the event. Now, by way of contrast, let us take the montage of the stone lions in *The End of St. Petersburg.* By skillful juxtaposition a group of sculptured lions are made to look like a single lion getting to its feet, a symbol of the aroused masses. This clever device would be unthinkable in any film after 1932. As late as 1935 Fritz Lang, in *Fury,* followed a series of shots of women scandalmongering with shots of clucking chickens in a farmyard. This relic of associative montage came as a shock even at the time, and today seems entirely out of keeping with the rest of the film. However decisive the art of Marcel Carné, for example, in our estimate of the respective values of *Quai des Brumes* or of *Le Jour se lève* his editing remains on the level of the reality he is analyzing. There is only one proper way of looking at it. That is why we are witnessing the almost complete disappearance of optical effects such as superimpositions, and even, especially in the United States, of the close-up, the too violent impact of which would make the audience conscious of the cutting. In the typical American comedy the director returns as often as he can to a shot of the characters from the knees up, which is said to be best suited to catch the spontaneous attention of the viewer—the natural point of balance of his mental adjustment.

Actually this use of montage originated with the silent movies. This is more or less the part it plays in Griffith's films, for example in *Broken Blossoms,* because with *Intolerance* he had already introduced that synthetic concept of montage which the Soviet cinema was to carry to its ultimate conclusion and which is to be found again, although less exclusively, at the end of the silent era. It is understandable, as a matter of fact, that the sound image, far less flexible than the visual image, would carry montage in the direction of realism, increasingly eliminating both plastic expressionism and the symbolic relation between images.

Thus around 1938 films were edited, almost without exception, according to the same principle. The story was unfolded in a series of set-ups numbering as a rule about 600. The characteristic procedure was by shot-reverse-shot, that is to say, in a dialogue scene, the camera followed the order of the text, alternating the character shown with each speech.

It was this fashion of editing, so admirably suitable for the best films made between 1930 and 1939, that was challenged by the shot in depth introduced by Orson Welles and William Wyler. The influence of *Citizen Kane* cannot be overestimated. Thanks to the depth of field, whole scenes are covered in one take, the camera remaining motionless. Dramatic effects for which we had formerly relied on montage were created out of the movements of the actors within a fixed framework. Of course Welles did not invent the in-depth shot any more than Griffith invented the close-up. All the pioneers used it and for a very good reason. Soft focus only appeared with montage. It was not only a technical must consequent upon the use of images in juxtaposition, it was a logical consequence of montage, its plastic equivalent. If at a given moment in the action the director, as in the scene imagined above, goes to a close-up of a bowl of fruit, it follows naturally that he also isolates it in space through the focusing of the lens. The soft focus of the background confirms therefore the effect of montage, that is to say, while it is of the essence of the storytelling, it is only an accessory of the style of the

33

photography. Jean Renoir had already clearly understood this, as we see from a statement of his made in 1938 just after he had made *La Bête humaine* and *La Grande illusion* and just prior to *La Règle du jeu:* "The more I learn about my trade the more I incline to direction in depth relative to the screen. The better it works, the less I use the kind of set-up that shows two actors facing the camera, like two well-behaved subjects posing for a still portrait." The truth of the matter is, that if you are looking for the precursor of Orson Welles, it is not Louis Lumière or Zecca, but rather Jean Renoir. In his films, the search after composition in depth is, in effect, a partial replacement of montage by frequent panning shots and entrances. It is based on a respect for the continuity of dramatic space and, of course, of its duration.

To anybody with eyes in his head, it is quite evident that the one-shot sequences used by Welles in *The Magnificent Ambersons* are in no sense the purely passive recording of an action shot within the same framing. On the contrary, his refusal to break up the action, to analyze the dramatic field in time, is a positive action the results of which are far superior to anything that could be achieved by the classical "cut."

All you need to do is compare two frames shot in depth, one from 1910, the other from a film by Wyler or Welles, to understand just by looking at the image, even apart from the context of the film, how different their functions are. The framing in the 1910 film is intended, to all intents and purposes, as a substitute for the missing fourth wall of the theatrical stage, or at least in exterior shots, for the best vantage point to view the action, whereas in the second case the setting, the lighting, and the camera angles give an entirely different reading. Between them, director and cameraman have converted the screen into a dramatic checkerboard, planned down to the last detail. The clearest if not the most original examples of this are to be found in *The Little Foxes* where the *mise-en-scène* takes on the severity of a working drawing. (Welles' pictures are more difficult to analyze because of his baroque excesses.) Objects and characters are related in such a fashion that it is impossible for the spectator to miss the significance of the scene. To get the same results by way of montage would have necessitated a detailed succession of shots.

What we are saying then is that the sequence of shots "in depth" of the contemporary director does not exclude the use of montage —how could he, without reverting to a primitive babbling?—he makes it an integral part of his "plastic." The storytelling of Welles or Wyler is no less explicit than John Ford's but theirs has the advantage over his that it does not sacrifice the specific effects that can be derived from unity of image in space and time. Whether an episode is analyzed bit by bit or presented in its physical entirety cannot surely remain a matter of indifference, at least in a work with some pretensions to style. It would obviously be absurd to deny that montage has added considerably to the progress of film language, but this has happened at the cost of other values, no less definitely cinematic.

This is why depth of field is not just a stock in trade of the cameraman like the use of a series of filters or of such-and-such a style of lighting, it is a capital gain in the field of direction—a dialectical step forward in the history of film language.

Nor is it just a formal step forward. Well used, shooting in depth is not just a more economical, a simpler, and at the same time a more subtle way of getting the most out of a scene. In addition to affecting the structure of film language, it also affects the relationships of the minds of the spectators to the image, and in consequence it influences the interpretation of the spectacle.

It would lie outside the scope of this article to analyze the psychological modalities of these relations, as also their aesthetic consequences, but it might be enough here to note, in general terms:

(1) That depth of focus brings the spectator into a relation with the image closer to that which he enjoys with reality. Therefore it is correct to say that, independently of the contents of the image, its structure is more realistic;

(2) That it implies, consequently, both a more active mental

attitude on the part of the spectator and a more positive contribution on his part to the action in progress. While analytical montage only calls for him to follow his guide, to let his attention follow along smoothly with that of the director who will choose what he should see, here he is called upon to exercise at least a minimum of personal choice. It is from his attention and his will that the meaning of the image in part derives.

(3) From the two preceding propositions, which belong to the realm of psychology, there follows a third which may be described as metaphysical. In analyzing reality, montage presupposes of its very nature the unity of meaning of the dramatic event. Some other form of analysis is undoubtedly possible but then it would be another film. In short, montage by its very nature rules out ambiguity of expression. Kuleshov's experiment proves this *per absurdum* in giving on each occasion a precise meaning to the expression on a face, the ambiguity of which alone makes the three successively exclusive expressions possible.

On the other hand, depth of focus reintroduced ambiguity into the structure of the image if not of necessity—Wyler's films are never ambiguous—at least as a possibility. Hence it is no exaggeration to say that *Citizen Kane* is unthinkable shot in any other way but in depth. The uncertainty in which we find ourselves as to the spiritual key or the interpretation we should put on the film is built into the very design of the image.

It is not that Welles denies himself any recourse whatsoever to the expressionistic procedures of montage, but just that their use from time to time in between one-shot sequences in depth gives them a new meaning. Formerly montage was the very stuff of cinema, the texture of the scenario. In *Citizen Kane* a series of superimpositions is contrasted with a scene presented in a single take, constituting another and deliberately abstract mode of storytelling. Accelerated montage played tricks with time and space while that of Welles, on the other hand, is not trying to deceive us; it offers us a contrast, condensing time, and hence is the equivalent for example of the French imperfect or the English frequentative tense. Like accelerated montage and montage of attractions these superimpositions, which the talking film had not used for ten years, rediscovered a possible use related to temporal realism in a film without montage.

If we have dwelt at some length on Orson Welles it is because the date of his appearance in the filmic firmament (1941) marks more or less the beginning of a new period and also because his case is the most spectacular and, by virtue of his very excesses, the most significant.

Yet *Citizen Kane* is part of a general movement, of a vast stirring of the geological bed of cinema, confirming that everywhere up to a point there had been a revolution in the language of the screen.

I could show the same to be true, although by different methods, of the Italian cinema. In Roberto Rossellini's *Paisà* and *Allemania Anno Zero* and Vittorio de Sica's *Ladri de Biciclette,* Italian neorealism contrasts with previous forms of film realism in its stripping away of all expressionism and in particular in the total absence of the effects of montage. As in the films of Welles and in spite of conflicts of style, neorealism tends to give back to the cinema a sense of the ambiguity of reality. The preoccupation of Rossellini when dealing with the face of the child in *Allemania Anno Zero* is the exact opposite of that of Kuleshov with the close-up of Mozhukhin. Rossellini is concerned to preserve its mystery. We should not be misled by the fact that the evolution of neorealism is not manifest, as in the United States, in any form of revolution in editing. They are both aiming at the same results by different methods. The means used by Rossellini and de Sica are less spectacular but they are no less determined to do away with montage and to transfer to the screen the *continuum* of reality. The dream of Zavattini is just to make a ninety-minute film of the life of a man to whom nothing ever happens. The most "aesthetic" of the neorealists, Luchino Visconti, gives just as clear a picture as Welles of the basic aim of his directorial art in *La Terra Trema,* a film almost entirely composed of one-shot sequences, thus clearly showing his concern to cover the entire action in interminable deep-focus panning shots.

However we cannot pass in review all the films that have shared in this revolution in film language since 1940. Now is the moment to attempt a synthesis of our reflections on the subject.

It seems to us that the decade from 1940 to 1950 marks a decisive step forward in the development of the language of the film. If we have appeared since 1930 to have lost sight of the trend of the silent film as illustrated particularly by Stroheim, F. W. Murnau, Robert Flaherty, and Dreyer, it is for a purpose. It is not that this trend seems to us to have been halted by the talking film. On the contrary, we believe that it represented the richest vein of the so-called silent film and, precisely because it was not aesthetically tied to montage, but was indeed the only tendency that looked to the realism of sound as a natural development. On the other hand it is a fact that the talking film between 1930 and 1940 owes it virtually nothing save for the glorious and retrospectively prophetic exception of Jean Renoir. He alone in his searchings as a director prior to *La Règle du jeu* forced himself to look back beyond the resources provided by montage and so uncovered the secret of a film form that would permit everything to be said without chopping the world up into little fragments, that would reveal the hidden meanings in people and things without disturbing the unity natural to them.

It is not a question of thereby belittling the films of 1930 to 1940, a criticism that would not stand up in the face of the number of masterpieces, it is simply an attempt to establish the notion of a dialectic progress, the highest expression of which was found in the films of the 1940's. Undoubtedly, the talkie sounded the knell of a certain aesthetic of the language of film, but only wherever it had turned its back on its vocation in the service of realism. The sound film nevertheless did preserve the essentials of montage, namely discontinuous description and the dramatic analysis of action. What it turned its back on was metaphor and symbol in exchange for the illusion of objective presentation. The expressionism of montage has virtually disappeared but the relative realism of the kind of cutting that flourished around 1937 implied a congenital limitation which escaped us so long as it was perfectly suited to its subject matter. Thus American comedy reached its peak within the framework of a form of editing in which the realism of the time played no part. Dependent on logic for its effects, like vaudeville and plays on words, entirely conventional in its moral and sociological content, American comedy had everything to gain, in strict line-by-line progression, from the rhythmic resources of classical editing.

Undoubtedly it is primarily with the Stroheim-Murnau trend—almost totally eclipsed from 1930 to 1940—that the cinema has more or less consciously linked up once more over the last ten years. But it has no intention of limiting itself simply to keeping this trend alive. It draws from it the secret of the regeneration of realism in storytelling and thus of becoming capable once more of bringing together real time, in which things exist, along with the duration of the action, for which classical editing had insidiously substituted mental and abstract time. On the other hand, so far from wiping out once and for all the conquests of montage, this reborn realism gives them a body of reference and a meaning. It is only an increased realism of the image that can support the abstraction of montage. The stylistic repertory of a director such as Hitchcock, for example, ranged from the power inherent in the basic document as such, to superimpositions, to large close-ups. But the close-ups of Hitchcock are not the same as those of C. B. de Mille in *The Cheat* [1915]. They are just one type of figure, among others, of his style. In other words, in the silent days, montage evoked what the director wanted to say; in the editing of 1938, it described it. Today we can say that at last the director writes in film. The image—its plastic composition and the way it is set in time, because it is founded on a much higher degree of realism—has at its disposal more means of manipulating reality and of modifying it from within. The film-maker is no longer the competitor of the painter and the playwright, he is, at last, the equal of the novelist.

THE VIRTUES AND LIMITATIONS OF MONTAGE

(Montage Interdit. Crin Blanc. Le Ballon Rouge. Une Fée pas comme les autres.)

THE CREATIVE originality of A. Lamorisse was already apparent in *Bim, le petit âne*. *Bim* and perhaps *Crin Blanc* are the only two real children's films ever made. Of course there are others— although not as many as one would expect—that are suited to a variety of young age groups. The Soviet Union has made special efforts in this field but it is my feeling that films like *Lone White Sails* are already aimed at young adolescents. The attempts of J. Arthur Rank at specialized production in this area have failed both aesthetically and commercially. In fact, anyone wishing to set up a film library or to compile a series of programs for young children would be hard pressed to find more than a few shorts, of unequal merit, and a certain number of commercial films, among them some cartoons, the inspiration and the subject matter of which were sufficiently childlike; in particular, certain adventure films. It is not, however, a matter of specialized production, just of films intelligible to those on a mental level under fourteen. As we know, American films do not often rise above this level. The same is true of the animation films of Walt Disney.

It is obvious that films of this sort are in no way comparable to children's literature properly so called, and of which there is anyhow not a great deal. Before the disciples of Freud came on the scene, J.-J. Rousseau had already noted that this literature was not without offense. La Fontaine is a cynical moralist, the Countess of Ségur is a diabolical, sadomasochistic grandmother. It is now admitted that the *Tales of Perrault* conceal highly unmentionable symbols and one must concede that it is difficult to counter the arguments of the psychoanalysts. All the same, it is certainly not necessary to employ psychoanalysis to discover the delicious and terrifying profundities that are the source of the beauty of *Alice in Wonderland* and the fairy tales of Hans Christian Andersen. These authors had a capacity for dreaming that was equal in kind and intensity to that of a child. There is nothing puerile about that imaginary world. It was pedagogy that invented harmless colors for children, but to see the use they make of them is to find your gaze riveted on green paradises peopled with monsters.

The authors of genuine children's literature, then, are only rarely and indirectly educators . . . Jules Verne is perhaps the only one. They are poets whose imagination is privileged to remain on the dream wavelength of childhood.

That is why it is always easy to argue that their works are in a way harmful and really only suitable for grownups. If what we mean by that is that they are not edifying, this is true, but it is a pedagogic point of view, not an aesthetic one. On the other hand, the fact that adults enjoy them even perhaps more than children is a proof of their authenticity and value. The artist who works spontaneously for children has attained a quality of universality.

Le Ballon Rouge is already perhaps a little on the intellectual side and to that extent less childlike. The symbol appears in clearer outline in the myth, like a watermark. Nevertheless, to compare it with *Une Fée pas comme les autres* is to bring out, to a marked degree, the difference between poetry that is valid both for grownups and children and the childlike things suitable only for children.

But it is not from this point of view that I wish to discuss them. This article is not strictly speaking a critical study and I shall refer only incidentally to the artistic qualities that I consider belong to these works. My intention will be, on the basis of the astonishingly significant example that they provide, to make a simple analysis of certain rules of montage as they relate to cinematic expression, and more specifically still, of its aesthetic ontology. From this point of view, on the contrary, the similarities of *Ballon Rouge* and *Une Fée pas comme les autres* could very well have been premeditated. Both are marvellous demonstrations, in exactly opposite ways, of the virtues and the limitations of montage.

I shall begin with the film by Jean Tourane and show what an extraordinary illustration it is of the famous experiment of Kuleshov with the close-up of Mozhukhin. As we know, the naive ambition of Jean Tourane is to make Disney pictures with live animals. Now it is quite obvious that the human feelings we attribute to animals are, essentially at any rate, a projection of our own awareness. We simply read into their looks or into their behavior those states of mind that we claim they possess because of certain outward resemblances to us, or certain patterns of behavior which seem to resemble our own. We should not disregard or underestimate this perfectly natural tendency of the human mind, which has been harmful only in the realm of science. Indeed it is worth noting that today science, as a result of experiments carried out by distinguished investigators, has rediscovered a measure of truth in anthropomorphism. An example of this is the language of bees which, as tested and interpreted by the entomologist Von Frisch, goes far beyond the wildest analogies of the most unrepentant anthropomorphist. In any event, the margin of error is greater on the side of Descartes and his animal-machine than of Buffon and his half-human animals. But over and above this elementary aspect, it is quite evident that anthropomorphism derives from a form of analogical knowledge that psychological investigation cannot explain, still less refute. Its domain extends then from morality (the fables of La Fontaine) to the highest form of religious symbolism, by way of every region of magic and poetry.

You cannot therefore condemn anthropomorphism out of hand and not take into consideration the level it is on. One is forced to admit however that in the case of Jean Tourane it is on the lowest level. At once the most scientifically unsound and the least aesthetically adapted, if his work can claim any indulgence, it is on the grounds that its quantitative importance allows us to a staggering extent to explore the comparative possibilities of anthropomorphism and montage. Thus the cinema can actually multiply the static interpretations of photography by those that derive from the juxtaposition of shots.

For it is very important to note that Tourane's animals are not tamed, only gentled. Nor do they ever actually do the things they seem to be doing. When they do, it is by a trick, either with a hand offscreen guiding them, or an artificial paw like a marionette on a string. All Tourane's ingenuity and talent lies in his ability to get the animals to stay put in the positions in which he has placed them for the duration of the take. The environment, the dissimulation, the commentary are already sufficient to give to the bearing of the animal an almost human quality which, in turn, the illusion of montage underlines and magnifies to such an extent that at times it makes the impression almost complete. In this way, without the protagonists having done anything beyond remaining perfectly still in front of the camera, a whole story is built up with a large number of characters in complicated relationships—often so complex that the scenario is confused—and all with a wide variety of characteristics. The apparent action and the meaning we attribute to it do not exist, to all intents and purposes, prior to the assembling of the film, not even in the form of fragmented scenes out of which the setups are generally composed. I will go further and say that, in the circumstances, the use of montage was not just one way of making this film, it was the *only* way. Actually if Tourane's animals were as intelligent say as Rin-Tin-Tin and able to do for themselves, as a result of training, the bulk of the things that montage here credits them with doing, the focus of the film would be radically altered. We would no longer be concerned with the story but rather with the skill of the animals. In other words, it would pass from being something imaginary to something real. Instead of delighting in a fiction, we would be full of admiration for a well-executed vaudeville turn. It is montage, that abstract creator of meaning, which preserves the state of unreality demanded by the spectacle.

The opposite is true of *Le Ballon Rouge*. It is my view, and I shall prove it, that this film ought not to, nor can it, owe anything to montage. This is all the more of a paradox since the zoomorphism of the balloon is even more an affair of the imagination than the anthropomorphism of the animals. Lamorisse's red balloon actually does go through the movements in front of the camera that we see on the screen. Of course there is a trick in it, but it is not one that belongs to cinema as such. Illusion is created here, as in conjuring, out of reality itself. It is something concrete, and does not derive from the potential extensions created by montage.

What does it matter, you will say, provided the result is the same—if, for example, we are made to accept on the screen the existence of a balloon that can follow its master like a little dog? It matters to this extent, that with montage the magic balloon would exist only on the screen, whereas that of Lamorisse sends us back to reality.

Perhaps we should digress here for a moment and point out that by nature montage is not something absolute, at least psychologically speaking. In its original, simple form, people did not see it as an artifice any more than did those people at the first showing of Lumière's film who rushed to the back of the room when the train entered the station at Ciotat. But the habit of cinema-going has gradually alerted audiences and today a sizable portion of the public, if you asked them to concentrate a little, would be able to distinguish between real scenes and those created by montage. It is a fact that other devices such as process shots make it possible for two objects, say the star and a tiger, to be seen together, a proximity which if it were real might cause some problems. The illusion here is more complete, but it can be detected and in any case, the important thing is not whether the trick can be spotted but whether or not trickery is used, just as the beauty of a copy is no substitute for the authenticity of a Vermeer. Some will object that there is trickery in the handling of Lamorisse's balloon. Of course there is, otherwise we would be watching the documentary of a miracle or of a fakir at work and that would be quite another kind of film. *Ballon Rouge* is a tale told in film, a pure creation of the mind, but the important thing about it is that this story owes everything to the cinema precisely because, essentially, it owes it nothing.

It is very easy to imagine *Ballon Rouge* as a literary tale. But no matter how delightfully written, the book could never come up to the film, the charm of which is of another kind. Nevertheless, the same story no matter how well filmed might not have had a greater measure of reality on the screen than in the book, supposing that Lamorisse had had recourse either to the illusions of montage or, failing that, to process work. The film would then be a tale told image by image—as is the story, word by word—instead of being what it is, namely *the picture of a story* or, if you prefer, an imaginary documentary.

This expression seems to me once and for all to be the one that best defines what Lamorisse was attempting, namely something like, yet different from, the film that Cocteau created in *Le Sang d'un poète,* that is to say, a documentary on the imagination, in other words, on the dream. Here we are then, caught up by our thinking in a series of paradoxes. Montage which we are constantly being told is the essence of cinema is, in this situation, the literary and anticinematic process *par excellence*. Essential cinema, seen for once in its pure state, on the contrary, is to be found in straightforward photographic respect for the unity of space.

Now we must take our analysis a little farther, since it might with reason be pointed out that while *Ballon Rouge* owes nothing essentially to montage, it depends on it accidentally. For, if Lamorisse spent 500,000 francs on red balloons, it was because he wanted to be sure he would not lack doubles. Similarly, the horse Crin Blanc was doubly a myth since several horses, all looking the same, all more or less wild, were shown on the screen as a single horse. This observation will allow us to give an even more precise definition of an essential law of film stylistics.

It would be a betrayal of Lamorisse's films, for example *Le Rideau cramoisi,* to call them works of pure fiction. Their believability is undoubtedly tied in with their documentary value. The events they portray are partially true. The countryside of the Camargue, the lives of the horse-breeders and the fishermen, the habits of the herds, constitute the basis for the story of *Crin Blanc,* providing a firm and unshakable support for the myth. But it is precisely on this reality that a dialectic belonging to the realm of the imaginary, and interestingly symbolized by the use of doubles for Crin Blanc, is founded. Thus Crin Blanc is at one and the same time a real horse that grazes on the salty grass of the Camargue and a dream horse swimming eternally at the side of little Folco. Its cinematic reality could not do without its documentary reality, but if it is to become a truth of the imagination, it must die and be born again of reality itself.

Undoubtedly, the shooting of the film called for a variety of skills. The little boy that Lamorisse chose had never been near a horse, yet he had to be taught to ride bareback. A number of scenes were shot virtually without the help of trick work and certainly with a considerable disregard for very real dangers. Yet a moment's reflection is enough to show that if what we see depicted had been really the truth, successfully created in front of the camera, the film would cease to exist because it would cease, by the same token, to be a myth. It is that fringe of trick work, that margin of subterfuge demanded by the logic of the story that allows what is imaginary to include what is real and at the same time to substitute for it. If there had only been one wild horse painfully subjected to the demands of the camera, the film would have been just a tour de force, an exhibition of successful training like Tom Mix and his white horse.

It is clear what we would lose by this. If the film is to fulfill itself aesthetically we need to believe in the reality of what is happening while knowing it to be tricked. Obviously the spectator does not have to know that there were three or even four horses * or that someone had to pull on a cotton thread to get the horse to turn its head at the right moment. All that matters is that the spectator can say at one and the same time that the basic material of the film is authentic while the film is also truly cinema. So the screen reflects the ebb and flow of our imagination which feeds on a reality for which it plans to substitute. That is to say, the tale is born of an experience that the imagination transcends.

Correspondingly, however, what is imaginary on the screen must have the spatial density of something real. You cannot therefore use montage here except within well-defined limits or you run the risk of threatening the very ontology of the cinematographic tale. For example, a director is not allowed to dodge the difficulty of showing two simultaneous aspects of an action by simply using shot-and-reverse-shot. Lamorisse in the scene of the rabbit hunt has shown that he clearly understood this. The horse, the boy, and the rabbit are all in the same shot together. However he came near to making a mistake in the scene of the capture of Crin Blanc when the boy is letting himself be dragged along by the horse. It is of no consequence that the horse we see dragging Folco in the long shot is a double for Crin Blanc, nor even that for that dangerous shot, Lamorisse had himself doubled for the boy, but I am embarrassed that at the end of the sequence when the horse slows down and finally

---

* In the same way, apparently, Rin-Tin-Tin owes his cinematic existence to several Alsatians who look like him and are all trained to do all the tricks that "only Rin-Tin-Tin" can do on the screen. Every one of these actions has to be completed in reality and without recourse to montage, the latter being used only in a secondary sense, in order to contribute to the imaginary power of the myth of some very real dogs, all of whose qualities Rin-Tin-Tin possesses.

stops, the camera does not show us, so that we are in no doubt about it, that the horse and child are in physical proximity. This could have been done in a panning shot or by pulling the camera back. This simple precautionary shot would in retrospect have authenticated all that had preceded it. To show two separate shots of Folco and the horse dodges a problem, albeit at this stage of the action with less harmful results, and thereby interrupts the lovely spatial flow of the action.*

---

* Perhaps I shall make myself clearer by giving an example. In an otherwise mediocre English film, *Where No Vultures Fly,* there is one unforgettable sequence. The film reconstructs the story of a young couple in South Africa during the war who founded and organized a game reserve. To this end, husband and wife, together with their child, lived in the heart of the bush. The sequence I have in mind starts out in the most conventional way. Unknown to its parents, the child has wandered away from the camp and has found a lion cub that has been temporarily abandoned by its mother. Unaware of the danger, it picks up the cub and takes it along. Meanwhile the lioness, alerted either by the noise or by the scent of the child, turns back towards its den and starts along the path taken by the unsuspecting child. She follows close behind him. The little group comes within sight of the camp at which point the distracted parents see the child and the lion which is undoubtedly about to spring at any moment on the imprudent kidnapper. Here let us interrupt the story for a moment. Up to this point everything has been shown in parallel montage and the somewhat naive attempt at suspense has seemed quite conventional. Then suddenly, to our horror, the director abandons his montage of separate shots that has kept the protagonists apart and gives us instead parents, child, and lioness all in the same full shot. This single frame in which trickery is out of the question gives immediate and retroactive authenticity to the very banal montage that has preceded it. From then on, and always in the same full shot, we see the father order his son to stand still—the lion has halted a few yards away—then to put the cub down on the ground and to start forward again without hurrying. Whereupon the lion comes quietly forward, picks up the cub and moves off into the bush while the overjoyed parents rush towards the child.

It is obvious that, considered from the point of view of a recital, this sequence would have had the same simple meaning if it had been shot entirely in montage or by process work. But in neither event would the scene have unfolded before the camera in its physical and spatial reality. Hence, in spite of the concrete nature of each shot, it would have had the impact only of a story and not of a real event. There would have been no difference between the scene as shot and the chapter in a novel which recounted the same imaginary episode. Hence the dramatic and moral values of the episode would be on a very mediocre level. On the other hand, the final framing which involved putting the characters in a real situation carries us at once to the heights of cinematographic emotion. Naturally the feat was made possible by the fact that the lioness was half tamed and had been living before the filming in close con-

If one forced oneself at this point to define the problem, it seems to me that one could set up the following principle as a law of aesthetics. "When the essence of a scene demands the simultaneous presence of two or more factors in the action, montage is ruled out." It can reclaim its right to be used, however, whenever the import of the action no longer depends on physical contiguity even though this may be implied. For example, it was all right for Lamorisse to show, as he did, the head of the horse in close-up, turning obediently in the boy's direction, but he should have shown the two of them in the same frame in the preceding shot.

It is in no sense a question of being obliged to revert to a single-shot sequence or of giving up resourceful ways of expressing things or convenient ways of varying the shots. Our concern here is not with the form but with the nature of the recital of events—or to be more precise with a certain interdependence of nature and form. When Orson Welles deals with certain scenes in *The Magnificent Ambersons* in a single shot whereas in *Mr. Arkadin* he uses a finely broken-down montage, it is only a change of style and in no essential way alters the subject matter. I would even say that Hitchcock's *Rope* could just as well have been cut in the classic way whatever artistic importance may be correctly attached to the way he actually handled it. On the other hand it is inconceivable that the famous seal-hunt scene in *Nanook* should not show us hunter, hole, and seal all in the same shot. It is simply a question of respect for the spatial unity of an event at the moment when to split it up would change it from something real into something imaginary. Flaherty as a rule understood this, except in a few places where, as a consequence, there is a failure of consistency. While the picture of Nanook hunting seal on the rim of an ice hole is one of the loveliest

---

tact with the family. This is not the point. The question is not whether the child really ran the risk it seemed to run but that the episode was shot with due respect for its spatial unity. Realism here resides in the homogeneity of space. Thus we see that there are cases in which montage far from being the essence of cinema is indeed its negation. The same scene then can be poor literature or great cinema according to whether montage or a full shot is used.

in all cinema, the scene of the struggle with the alligator on a fishing line in *Louisiana Story,* obviously montage, is weak. On the other hand, the scene in the same film of an alligator catching a heron, photographed in a single panning shot, is admirable.

However, the reciprocal fact is also true. That is to say, to restore reality to a recital of events it is sufficient if one of the shots, suitably chosen, brings together those elements previously separated off by montage. It is not easy however to state offhand to what kind of subject or in what circumstances this applies. I will confine myself, prudently, to just a few indications. First of all, it is naturally true of all documentary films, the object of which is to present facts which would cease to be interesting if the episodes did not actually occur in front of the camera, that is to say in documentary films that approximate to reporting. Newsreels may also be included up to a point. The fact that reconstructions of actual events were acceptable in the earliest days of the cinema is a clear indication that there has been an evolution in the attitude of the general public.

The same rule does not apply to didactic documentaries, the purpose of which is not to report but to explain an event. Of course in these, too, there is a place for sequences of the first type of documentary. Take, for example, a documentary about conjuring! If its object is to show the extraordinary feats of a great master then the film must proceed in a series of individual shots, but if the film is required subsequently to explain one of these tricks, it becomes necessary to edit them. The case is clear, so let us move on!

A much more interesting example is that of the fiction film, ranging from the fairytale world of *Crin Blanc* to the mildly romanticized type of documentary such as *Nanook.* It is a question then, as we have said above, of fictions that do not derive their full significance or, at most, only derive their value, from the integration of the real and the imaginary. It is the aspects of this reality that dictate the cutting.

Finally, in the case of narrative films that parallel the novel or

51

the play, it is probable that certain kinds of action are not adapted to montage for their full development. The expression of concrete duration conflicts with the abstract time of montage as *Citizen Kane* and *Ambersons* so well illustrate. Above all, certain situations can only be said to exist cinematographically to the extent that their spatial unity is established, especially comedy situations that are based on the relations between human beings and things. As in *Ballon Rouge,* every kind of trick is permissible except montage. The primitive slapstick comedies, especially those of Keaton, and the films of Chaplin, have much to teach us on this score. If slapstick comedy succeeded before the days of Griffith and montage, it is because most of its gags derived from a comedy of space, from the relation of man to things and to the surrounding world. In *The Circus* Chaplin is truly in the lion's cage and both are enclosed within the framework of the screen.

IN DEFENSE OF MIXED CINEMA

A BACKWARD glance over the films of the past 10 or 15 years quickly reveals that one of the dominant features of their evolution is the increasingly significant extent to which they have gone for their material to the heritage of literature and the stage.

Certainly it is not only just now that the cinema is beginning to look to the novel and the play for its material. But its present approach is different. The adaptation of *Monte Cristo, Les Misérables,* or *Les Trois Mousquetaires* is not in the same category as that of *Symphonie pastorale, Jacques le fataliste, Les Dames du Bois de Boulogne, Le Diable au corps,* or *Le Journal d'un curé de campagne.* Alexandre Dumas and Victor Hugo simply serve to supply the film-maker with characters and adventures largely independent of their literary framework. Javert or D'Artagnan have become part of a mythology existing outside of the novels. They enjoy in some measure an autonomous existence of which the original works are no longer anything more than an accidental and almost superfluous manifestation. On the other hand, film-makers continue to adapt novels that are sometimes first-rate as novels but which they feel justified in treating simply as very detailed film synopses. Film-makers likewise go to novelists for character, a plot, even—and this is a further stage—for atmosphere, as for example from Simenon, or the poetic atmosphere found in Pierre Véry. But here again, one can ignore the fact that it is a book and just consider the writer a particularly prolix scenarist. This is so true that a great number of American crime novels are clearly written with a double purpose in view, namely with an eye on a Hollywood adaptation. Furthermore, respect for crime fiction when it shows any measure of originality is becoming more and more the rule; liberties cannot be taken with the author's text with an easy conscience. But when Robert Bresson says, before making *Le Journal d'un curé de campagne* into a film, that he is going to follow the book page by page, even phrase by phrase, it is clearly a question of something quite different and new values are involved. The cinéaste is no longer content, as were Corneille, La Fontaine or Molière before him, to ransack other works. His method is to bring to the screen virtually unaltered any work the excellence of which he decides on a priori. And how can it be otherwise when this work derives from a form of literature so highly developed that the heroes and the meaning of their actions depend very closely on the style of the author, when they are intimately wrapped up with it as in a microcosm, the laws of which, in themselves rigorously determined, have no validity outside that world, when the novel has renounced its epic-like simplicity so that it is no longer a matrix of myths but rather a locus of subtle interactions between style, psychology, morals, or metaphysics.

In the theater the direction of this evolution is more evident still. Dramatic literature, like the novel, has always allowed itself to suffer violence at the hands of the cinema. But who would dare to compare Laurence Olivier's *Hamlet* to the, in retrospect, ludicrous borrowings that the *film d'art* made once upon a time from the repertoire of the Comédie Française? It has always been a temptation to the film-maker to film theater since it is already a spectacle; but we know what comes of it. And it is with good reason that the term "filmed theater" has become a commonplace of critical opprobrium. The novel at least calls for some measure of creativity, in its transition from page to screen. The theater by contrast is a false friend; its illusory likeness to the cinema set the latter en route to a dead end, luring it onto the slippery slope of the merely facile. If the dramatic repertory of the boulevards, however, has occasionally been the source of a goodish film, that is only because the director has taken the same kind of liberty with the play as he would with a novel, retaining in fact only the characters and the plot. But there again, the phenomenon is radically new and this seems to imply respect for the theatrical character of the model as an inviolable principle.

The films we have just referred to and others the titles of which will undoubtedly be cited shortly, are both too numerous and of too high a quality to be taken as exceptions that prove the rule. On the contrary, works of this kind have for the last 10 years signposted the way for one of the most fruitful trends of contemporary cinema.

"Ça, c'est du cinéma!" "That's really cinema!" Georges Altmann long ago proclaimed from the cover of a book dedicated to the glorification of the silent film, from *The Pilgrim* to *The General Line*. Are the dogmas and hopes of the earliest film criticism that fought for the autonomy of the Seventh Art now to be discarded like an old hat? Is the cinema or what remains of it incapable of surviving without the twin crutches of literature and theater? Is it in process of becoming an art derived from and dependent on one of the traditional arts?

The question proposed for our consideration is not so new; first of all, it is the problem of the reciprocal influence of the arts and of adaptations in general. If the cinema were two or three thousand years old we would undoubtedly see more clearly that it does not lie outside the common laws of the evolution of the arts. But cinema is only sixty years old and already its historical perspectives are prodigiously blurred. What ordinarily extends through one or two civilizations is here contained within the life span of a single man.

Nor is this the principal cause of error, because this accelerated evolution is in no sense contemporary with that of the other arts. The cinema is young, but literature, theater, and music are as old as history. Just as the education of a child derives from imitating the adults around him, so the evolution of the cinema has been influenced by the example of the hallowed arts. Thus its history, from the beginning of the century on, is the result of determinants specific to the evolution of all art, and likewise of effects on it of the arts that have already evolved. Again, the confused pattern of this aesthetic complex is aggravated by certain sociological factors. The cinema, in fact, has come to the fore as the only popular art at a time when the theater, the social art *par excellence,* reaches only a privileged cultural or monied minority. It may be that the past 20 years of the cinema will be reckoned in its overall history as the equivalent of five centuries in literature. It is not a long history for an art, but it is for our critical sense. So let us try and narrow the field of these reflections.

First of all let it be said that adaptations which the modern critic looks upon as a shameful way out are an established feature of the history of art. Malraux has pointed out how much the painting of the Renaissance was originally indebted to Gothic sculpture. Giotto painted in full relief. Michelangelo deliberately refused any assistance he might have had from oils, the fresco being more suitable to a style of painting based on sculpture. And doubtless this was a stage quickly passed through on the way to the liberation of "pure painting." But would you therefore say that Giotto is inferior to Rembrandt? And what is the value of such a hierarchy? Can anyone deny that fresco in full relief was a necessary stage in the process of development and hence aesthetically justified? What again does one say about Byzantine miniatures in stone enlarged to the dimensions of a cathedral tympanum? And to turn now to the field of the novel, should one censure preclassical tragedy for adapting the pastoral novel for the stage or Madame La Fayette for her indebtedness to Racinian dramaturgy? Again, what is true technically is even truer of themes which turn up in all kinds and varieties of expression. This is a commonplace of literary history up to the eighteenth century, when the notion of plagiarism appeared for the first time. In the Middle Ages, the great Christian themes are to be found alike in theater, painting, stained-glass windows, and so on.

Doubtless what misleads us about the cinema is that, in contrast to what usually happens in the evolutionary cycle of an art, adaptation, borrowing, and imitation do not appear in the early stages. On the contrary, the autonomy of the means of expression, and the originality of subject matter, have never been greater than they were in the first twenty or thirty years of the cinema. One would expect a nascent art to try to imitate its elders and then, bit by bit, to work out its own laws and select its rightful themes. One finds it less easy to understand that it should place an increased volume of experience at the service of material foreign to its genius, as if its capacity for invention was in inverse proportion to its powers of expression. From there to the position that this paradoxical evolution is a form of decadence is but a step, and one that criticism did not hesitate to take upon the advent of sound.

But this was to misunderstand the basic facts of the history of film. The fact that the cinema appeared after the novel and the theater does not mean that it falls into line behind them and on the same plane. Cinema developed under sociological conditions very different from those in which the traditional arts exist. You might as well derive the *bal-musette* or bebop from classical choreography. The first film-makers effectively extracted what was of use to them from the art with which they were about to win their public, namely the circus, the provincial theater, and the music hall, which provided slapstick films, especially, with both technique and actors. Everyone is familiar with the saying attributed to Zecca when he discovered a certain Shakespeare. "What a lot of good stuff that character passed up!" Zecca and his fellows were in no danger of being influenced by a literature that neither they nor their audience read. On the other hand they were greatly influenced by the popular literature of the time, to which we owe the sublime *Fantômas,* one of the masterpieces of the screen. The film gave a new life to the conditions out of which came an authentic and great popular art. It did not spurn the humbler and despised forms of the theater, of the fairground, or of the penny dreadful. True, the fine gentlemen of the Academy and of the Comédie Française did make an effort to adopt this child that had been brought up in the profession of its parents, but the failure of their efforts only emphasized the futility of this unnatural enterprise. The misfortune of *Oedipus* and *Hamlet* meant about as much to the cinema in its early days as "our ancestors the Gauls" do to Negro elementary school children in the African bush. Any interest or charm that these early films have for us is on a par with those pagan and naive interpretations practiced by savage tribes that have gobbled up their missionaries. If the obvious borrowings in France—Hollywood unashamedly pillaged the techniques and personnel of the Anglo-Saxon music hall—from what survived of the popular theater, of the fairgrounds, or the boulevard, did not create aesthetic disputes, it was primarily because as yet there was no film criticism properly so called. It was likewise because such reincarnations by these so-called inferior arts did not shock anybody. No one felt any call to defend them except the interested parties who had more knowledge of their trade than they had of filmological preconceptions.

When the cinema actually began to follow in the footsteps of the theater, a link was restored, after a century or two of evolution, with dramatic forms that had been virtually abandoned. Did those same learned historians who know everything there is to be known about farce in the sixteenth century ever make it their business to find out what a resurgence of vitality it had between 1910 and 1914 at the Pathé and Gaumont Studios and under the baton of Mack Sennett?

It would be equally easy to demonstrate that the same process occurred in the case of the novel. The serial film adopting the popular technique of the feuilleton revived the old forms of the *conte*. I experienced this personally when seeing once again

Feuillade's *Vampires* at one of those gatherings which my friend Henri Langlois, the director of the Cinémathèque Française, knows how to organize so well. That night only one of the two projectors was working. In addition, the print had no subtitles and I imagine that Feuillade himself would have had difficulty in trying to recognize the murderers. It was even money as to which were the good guys and which the bad. So difficult was it to tell who was which that the apparent villains of one reel turned out to be the victims in the next. The fact that the lights were turned on every ten minutes to change reels seemed to multiply the episodes. Seen under these conditions, Feuillade's *chef d'oeuvre* reveals the aesthetic principle that lies behind its charm. Every interruption evoked an "ah" of disappointment and every fresh start a sigh of hope for a solution. This story, the meaning of which was a complete mystery to the audience, held its attention and carried it along purely and simply by the tension created in the telling. There was no question of preexisting action broken up by intervals, but of a piece unduly interrupted, an inexhaustible spring, the flow of which was blocked by a mysterious hand. Hence the unbearable tension set up by the next episode to follow and the anxious wait, not so much for the events to come as for the continuation of the telling, of the restarting of an interrupted act of creation. Feuillade himself proceeded in the same way in making his films. He had no idea what would happen next and filmed step by step as the morning's inspiration came. Both the author and the spectator were in the same situation, namely, that of the King and Scheherazade; the repeated intervals of darkness in the cinema paralleled the separating off of the Thousand and One Nights. The "to be continued" of the true feuilleton as of the old serial films is not just a device extrinsic to the story. If Scheherazade had told everything at one sitting, the King, cruel as any film audience, would have had her executed at dawn. Both storyteller and film want to test the power of their magic by way of interruption, to know the teasing sense of waiting for the continuation of a tale that is a substitute for everyday living which, in its turn, is but a break in the continuity of a dream. So we see that the so-called original purity of the primitive screen does not stand up under examination. The sound film does not mark the threshold of a lost paradise on the other side of which the muse of the seventh art, discovering her nakedness, would then start to put back the rags of which she had been stripped. The cinema has not escaped a universal law. It has obeyed it in its own way—the only way possible, in view of the combination of technical and sociological circumstances affecting it.

We know of course that it is not enough to have proved that the greater part of the early films were only either borrowed or pillaged in order to justify thereby the actual form of that adaptation. Deprived of his usual stand the champion of pure cinema could still argue that intercourse between the arts is easier at the primitive level. It may very well be that farce is indebted to the cinema for its rejuvenation. But its effectiveness was primarily visual and it is by way of farce, first of all, and then of the music hall, that the old traditions of mime have been preserved. The farther one penetrates into the history of types, the more the differences become clear, just as in the evolution of animals at the extremities of the branches deriving from a common source. The original polyvalence having developed its potential, these are henceforth bound up with subtleties and complexities of form such that to attack them is to compromise the whole work itself. Under the direct influence of architectural sculpture Raphael and Da Vinci were already attacking Michelangelo for making painting a radically autonomous art.

There is some doubt that this objection could stand up under a detailed discussion, and that evolved forms do not continue to act on one another, but it is true that the history of art goes on developing in the direction of autonomy and specificity. The concept of pure art—pure poetry, pure painting, and so on—is not entirely without meaning; but it refers to an aesthetic reality as difficult to define as it is to combat. In any case, even if a certain mixing of the arts remains possible, like the mixing of genres, it does not necessarily follow that they are all fortunate mixtures. There are fruitful cross-breedings which add to the qualities derived from the parents; there are attractive but barren hybrids and there are likewise hideous combinations that bring forth nothing but chimeras. So let us stop appealing to precedents drawn from the origin of the cinema and let us take up again the problem as it seems to confront us today.

While critics are apt to view with regret the borrowings made by cinema from literature, the existence of a reverse process is as accepted as it is undeniable. It is in fact commonly agreed that the novel, and particularly the American novel, has come under the influence of the cinema. Let us leave to one side books in which the influence or direct borrowings are deliberate and so of little use for our purpose, as for example *Loin de Rueil* by Raymond Queneau. The question is whether or not the art of Dos Passos, Caldwell, Hemingway, or Malraux derives from the technique of the cinema. To tell the truth, we do not believe it for a moment. Undoubtedly, and how could it be otherwise, the new way of seeing things provided by the screen—seeing things in close-up or by way of storytelling forms such as montage—has helped the novelist to refurbish his technical equipment. But even where the relationship to cinematic techniques is avowed, they can at the same time be challenged: they are simply an addition to the apparatus available to the writer for use in the process of building his own particular world. Even if one admits that the novel has been somewhat shaped by the aesthetic gravitational pull of the cinema, this influence of a new art has unquestionably not been greater than that of the theater on literature during the last century. The influence of a dominant neighbor on the other arts is probably a constant law. Certainly, the work of Graham Greene seems to offer undeniable proof of this. But a closer look reveals that his so-called film techniques—we must not forget that he was a film critic for a number of years—are actually never used in the cinema. So marked is this that one is constantly asking oneself as one "visualizes" the author's style why film-makers continue to deprive themselves of a technique that could be so useful to them. The originality of a film such as *L'Espoir* by Malraux lies in its capacity to show us what the cinema would be if it took its inspiration from the novels "influenced" by the cinema. What should we conclude from this? Surely that we should rather reverse the usual theory and study the influence of modern literature on film-makers.

What do we actually mean by "cinema" in our present context? If we mean a mode of expression by means of realistic representation, by a simple registering of images, simply an outer seeing as opposed to the use of the resources of introspection or of analysis in the style of the classical novel, then it must be pointed out that the English novelists had already discovered in behaviorism the psychological justifications of such a technique. But here the literary critic is guilty of imprudently prejudging the true nature of cinema, based on a very superficial definition of what is here meant by reality. Because its basic material is photography it does not follow that the seventh art is of its nature dedicated to the dialectic of appearances and the psychology of behavior. While it is true that it relies entirely on the outside world for its objects it has a thousand ways of acting on the appearance of an object so as to eliminate any equivocation and to make of this outward sign one and only one inner reality. The truth is that the vast majority of images on the screen conform to the psychology of the theater or to the novel of classical analysis. They proceed from the commonsense supposition that a necessary and unambiguous causal relationship exists between feelings and their outward manifestations. They postulate that all is in the consciousness and that this consciousness can be known.

If, a little more subtly, one understands by cinema the techniques of a narrative born of montage and change of camera position, the same statement holds true. A novel by Dos Passos or Malraux is no less different from those films to which we are accustomed than it is from a novel by Fromentin or Paul Bourget.

Actually, the American novel belongs not so much to the age of cinema as to a certain vision of the world, a vision influenced doubtless by man's relations with a technical civilization, but whose influence upon the cinema, which is a fruit of this civilization, has been less than on the novel, in spite of the alibis that the film-maker can offer the novelist.

Likewise, in going to the novel the cinema has usually looked not as one might expect to works in which some have seen its influence already operating, but, in Hollywood, to Victorian literature and in France, to Henri Bordeaux and Pierre Benoît. Better . . . or worse . . . when an American director turns his attention on some rare occasion to a work by Hemingway, for example *For Whom the Bell Tolls,* he treats it in the traditional style that suits each and every adventure story.

The way things are, then, it would seem as if the cinema was fifty years behind the novel. If we maintain that the cinema influences the novel then we must suppose that it is a question of a potential image, existing exclusively behind the magnifying glass of the critic and seen only from where he sits. We would then be talking about the influence of a nonexistent cinema, an ideal cinema, a cinema that the novelist would produce if he were a film-maker; of an imaginary art that we are still awaiting.

And, God knows, this hypothesis is not as silly as it sounds. Let us hold on to it, at least as we do to those imaginary values which cancel one another out following on the equation that they have helped to solve.

If the apparent influence of the cinema on the novel has led the minds of some otherwise sound critics astray, it is because the novelist now uses narrative techniques and adopts a standard of evaluation of the facts, the affinity of which with the ways of the cinema are undoubted, whether borrowed directly, or as we prefer to think, of a certain aesthetic convergence that has simultaneously polarized several contemporary forms of expression. But in this process of influences or of resemblances, it is the novel which has proceeded most logically along the pathways of style. The novel it is that has made the subtlest use of montage, for example, and of the reversal of chronology. Above all it is the novel that has discovered the way to raise to the level of an authentic metaphysical significance an almost mirror-like objectivity. What camera has ever been as externally related to its object as the consciousness of the hero of Albert Camus' *L'Etranger?* The fact of the matter is that we do not know if *Manhattan Transfer* or *La Condition humaine* would have been very different without the cinema, but we are certain on the contrary that *Thomas Garner* and *Citizen Kane* would never have existed if it had not been for James Joyce and Dos Passos. We are witnessing, at the point at which the avant-garde has now arrived, the making of films that dare to take their inspiration from a novel-like style one might describe as ultracinematographic. Seen from this angle the question of borrowing is only of secondary importance. The majority of the films that we have presently in mind are not adaptations from novels yet certain episodes of *Paisà* are much more indebted to Hemingway (the scenes in the marshes), or to Saroyan (Naples) than Sam Wood's *For Whom The Bell Tolls* is to the original. By contrast, Malraux's film is the close equivalent of certain episodes in *L'Espoir* and the best of the recent English films are adaptations of Graham Greene. In our view the most satisfactory is the modestly made *Brighton Rock,* which passed almost unnoticed while John Ford was lost in the sumptuous falsification of *The Fugitive (The Power and the Glory).* Let us therefore see what the best contemporary films owe to the contemporary novelists— something it would be easy to demonstrate up to the appearance especially of *Ladri di Biciclette.* So, far from being scandalized by adaptations, we shall see in them, if not alas a certain augury for the progress of cinema, at least a possible factor in this progress, to the extent, at least, that the novelist transforms it. Perhaps you may say that this is all very true about modern novels, if the cinema is simply recouping here a hundredfold what it has already lent to the novel, but what is the argument worth when the film-maker pretends he is taking his inspiration from Gide or Stendhal? And why not from Proust or even from Madame de La Fayette?

And indeed why not? Jacques Bourgeois in an article in *La Revue du Cinéma* has made a brilliant analysis of the affinities between *A La Recherche du temps perdu* and cinematic forms of expression. Actually, the real problems to be faced in discussing the theories of such adaptations do not belong to the realm of aesthetics. They do not derive from the cinema as an art form but as a sociological and industrial fact. The drama of adaptation is the drama of popularization. A provincial publicity blurb on *La Chartreuse de Parme* described it as taken from "the famous cloak-and-dagger novel." We sometimes get the truth from film salesmen who have never read Stendhal. Shall we therefore condemn the film by Christian Jacque? Yes, to the extent that he has been false to the essence of the novel and wherever we feel that this betrayal was not inevitable. No, if we take into consideration first of all that this adaptation is above the average film level in quality and secondly that, all things considered, it provides an enchanting introduction to Stendhal's work and has certainly increased the number of its readers. It is nonsense to wax wroth about the indignities practiced on literary works on the screen, at least in the name of literature. After all, they cannot harm the original in the eyes of those who know it, however little they approximate to it. As for those who are unacquainted with the original, one of two things may happen; either they will be satisfied with the film which is as good as most, or they will want to know the original, with the resulting gain for literature. This argument is supported by publishers' statistics that show a rise in the sale of literary works after they have been adapted to the screen. No, the truth is, that culture in general and literature in particular have nothing to lose from such an enterprise.

There now remains the cinema, and I personally feel that there is every reason to be concerned over the way it is too often used in relation to our literary capital because the film-maker has everything to gain from fidelity. Already much more highly developed, and catering to a relatively cultured and exacting public, the novel offers the cinema characters that are much more complex and, again, as regards the relation of form and content, a firmness of treatment and a subtlety to which we are not accustomed on the screen. Obviously if the material on which the scenarist and the director are working is in itself on an intellectual level higher than that usual in the cinema then two things can be done. Either this difference in level and the artistic prestige of the original work serves as a guarantee, a reservoir of ideas and a *cachet* for the film, as is the case with *Carmen, La Chartreuse de Parme,* or *L'Idiot,* or the film-makers honestly attempt an integral equivalent, they try at least not simply to use the book as an inspiration, not merely to adapt it, but to translate it onto the screen as instanced in *La Symphonie Pastorale, Le Diable au corps, The Fallen Idol,* or *Le Journal d'un curé de campagne.* We should not throw stones at the image-makers who simplify in adapting. Their betrayal as we have said is a relative thing and there is no loss to literature. But the hopes for the future of the cinema are obviously pinned to the second group. When one opens the sluice the level of the water is very little higher than that of the canal. When someone makes a film of *Madame Bovary* in Hollywood, the difference of aesthetic level between the work of Flaubert and the average American film being so great, the result is a standard American production that has only one thing wrong with it—that it is still called *Madame Bovary.* And how can it be otherwise when the literary work is brought face to face with the vast and powerful cinematographic industry: cinema is the great leveler. When, on the other hand, thanks to a happy combination of circumstances, the film-maker plans to treat the book as something different from a run-of-the-mill scenario, it is a little as if, in that moment, the whole of cinema is raised to the level of literature. This is the case with the *Madame Bovary* and *Une Partie de campagne* of Jean Renoir. Actually, these are not too very good examples, not because of the quality of the films but precisely because Renoir is more faithful to the spirit than the letter. What strikes us about the fidelity of Renoir is that paradoxically it is compatible with complete independence from the original. The justification for this is of course that the genius of Renoir is certainly as great as that of Flaubert or Maupassant. The phenomenon we face here is comparable then to the translation of Edgar Allan Poe by Baudelaire.

Certainly it would be better if all directors were men of genius; presumably then there would be no problem of adaptation. The critic is only too fortunate if he is confronted merely with men of talent. This is enough however on which to establish our thesis. There is nothing to prevent us from dreaming of a *Diable au corps* directed by Jean Vigo but let us congratulate ourselves that at least we have an adaptation by Claude Autant-Lara. Faithfulness to the work of Radiguet has not only forced the screenwriters to offer us interesting and relatively complex characters, it has incited them to flout some of the moral conventions of the cinema, to take certain risks—prudently calculated, but who can blame them for this—with public prejudices. It has widened the intellectual and moral horizons of the audience and prepared the way for other films of quality. What is more, this is not all; and it is wrong to present fidelity as if it were necessarily a negative enslavement to an alien aesthetic. Undoubtedly the novel has means of its own—language not the image is its material, its intimate effect on the isolated reader is not the same as that of a film on the crowd in a darkened cinema—but precisely for these reasons the differences in aesthetic structure make the search for equivalents an even more delicate matter, and thus they require all the more power of invention and imagination from the film-maker who is truly attempting a resemblance. One might suggest that in the realm of language and style cinematic creation is in direct ratio to fidelity. For the same reasons that render a word-by-word translation worthless and a too free translation a matter for condemnation, a good adaptation should result in a restoration of the essence of the letter and the spirit. But one knows how intimate a possession of a language and of the genius proper to it is required for a good translation. For example, taking the well-known simple past tenses of André Gide as being specifically a literary effect of a style, one might consider them subtleties that can never be translated into the cinema. Yet it is not at all certain that Delannoy in his *Symphonie pastorale* has not found the equivalent. The ever-present snow carries with it a subtle and polyvalent symbolism that quietly modifies the action, and provides it as it were with a permanent moral coefficient the value of which is not so different after all from that which the writer was searching for by the appropriate use of tenses. Yet, the idea of surrounding this spiritual adventure with snow and of ignoring systematically the summery aspect of the countryside is a truly cinematographic discovery, to which the director may have been led by a fortunate understanding of the text. The example of Bresson in *Le Journal d'un curé de campagne* is even more convincing; his adaptation reaches an almost dizzy height of fidelity by way of a ceaselessly created respect for the text. Alfred Beguin has rightly remarked that the violence characteristic of Bernanos could never have the same force in literature and cinema. The screen uses violence in such a customary fashion that it seems somehow like a devalued currency, which is at one and the same time provoking and conventional. Genuine fidelity to the tone set by the novelist calls thus for a kind of conversion of the violence of the text. The real equivalent of the hyperbole of Bernanos lay in the ellipsis and litotes of Robert Bresson's editing. The more important and decisive the literary qualities of the work, the more the adaptation disturbs its equilibrium, the more it needs a creative talent to reconstruct it on a new equilibrium not indeed identical with, but the equivalent of, the old one. To pretend that the adaptation of novels is a slothful exercise from which the true cinema, "pure cinema," can have nothing to gain, is critical nonsense to which all adaptations of quality give the lie. It is those who care the least for fidelity in the name of the so-called demands of the screen who betray at one and the same time both literature and the cinema.

The effective fidelity of a Cocteau or Wyler is not evidence of a backward step, on the contrary, it is evidence of a development of cinematographic intelligence. Whether it is, as with the author of *Les Parents terribles,* the astonishingly perspicacious mobility of the camera or, as with Wyler, the asceticism of his editing, the refining down of the photography, the use of the fixed camera and of deep focus, their success is the result of outstanding mastery; moreover it is evidence of an inventiveness of expression which is the exact opposite of a passive recording of theater. To show respect for the theater it is not enough to photograph it. To create theater of any worthwhile kind is more difficult than to create cinema and this is what the majority of adapters were trying to do up to now.

There is a hundred times more cinema, and better cinema at that, in one fixed shot in *The Little Foxes* or *Macbeth* than in all the exterior travelling shots, in all the natural settings, in all the geographical exoticism, in all the shots of the reverse side of the set, by means of which up to now the screen has ingeniously attempted to make us forget the stage. Far from being a sign of decadence, the mastering of the theatrical repertoire by the cinema is on the contrary a proof of maturity. In short, to adapt is no longer to betray but to respect. Let us take a comparison from circumstances in the material order. In order to attain this high level of aesthetic fidelity, it is essential that the cinematographic form of expression make progress comparable to that in the field of optics. The distance separating *Hamlet* from the *film d'art* is as great as that separating the complexities of the modern lens from the primitive condenser of the magic lantern. Its imposing complexity has no other purpose than to compensate for the distortions, the aberrations, the diffractions, for which the glass is responsible—that is to say, to render the *camera obscura* as objective as possible. The transition from a theatrical work to the screen demands, on the aesthetic level, a scientific knowledge, so to speak, of fidelity comparable to that of a camera operator in his photographic rendering. It is the termination of a progression and the beginning of a rebirth. If the cinema today is capable of effectively taking on the realm of the novel and the theater, it is primarily because it is sure enough of itself and master enough of its means so that it no longer need assert itself in the process. That is to say it can now aspire to fidelity—not the illusory fidelity of a replica—through an intimate understanding of its own true aesthetic structure which is a prerequisite and necessary condition of respect for the works it is about to make its own. The multiplication of adaptations of literary works which are far from cinematic need not disturb the critic who is concerned about the purity of the seventh art; on the contrary, they are the guarantee of its progress.

"Why then," it will be asked by those nostalgic for cinema with a capital C, independent, specific, autonomous, free of all compromise, "should so much art be placed at the service of a cause that does not need it—why make unauthentic copies of novels when one can read the book, and of *Phèdre* when all you need is to go to the Comédie Française? No matter how satisfying the adaptations may be, you cannot argue that they are worth more than the original, especially not of a film of an equal artistic quality on a theme that is specifically cinematographic? You cite *Le Diable au corps, The Fallen Idol, Les Parents terribles,* and *Hamlet.* Well and good. I can cite in return *The Gold Rush, Potemkin, Broken Blossoms, Scarface, Stagecoach,* or even *Citizen Kane,* all masterpieces which would never have existed without the cinema, irreplaceable additions to the patrimony of art. Even if the best of adaptations are no longer naive betrayals or an unworthy prostitution, it is still true that in them a great deal of talent has gone to waste. You speak of progress but progress which can only render the cinema sterile in making it an annex of literature. Give to the theater and to the novel that which is theirs and to the cinema that which can never belong elsewhere."

This last objection would be valid in theory if it did not overlook historical relativity, a factor to be counted when an art is in full evolution. It is quite true that an original scenario is preferable to an adaptation, all else being equal. No one dreams of contesting this. You may call Charlie Chaplin the Molière of the cinema, but we would not sacrifice *Monsieur Verdoux* for an adaptation of *Le Misanthrope*. Let us hope, then, to have as often as possible films like *Le Jour se lève, La Règle du jeu,* or *The Best Years of Our Lives.* But these are platonic wishes, attitudes of mind that have no bearing on the actual evolution of the cinema. If the cinema turns more and more to literature—indeed to painting or to drama—it is a fact which we take note of and attempt to understand because it is very likely that we cannot influence it. In such a situation, if fact does not absolutely make right, it requires the critic at least to be favorably predisposed. Once more, let us not be misled here by drawing an analogy with the other arts, especially those whose evolution towards an individualistic use has made virtually independent of the consumer. Lautréamont and Van Gogh produced their creative work while either misunderstood or ignored by their contemporaries. The cinema cannot exist without a minimum number, and it is an immense minimum, of people who frequent the cinema here and now. Even when the film-maker affronts the public taste there is no justification for his audacity, no justification except insofar as it is possible to admit that it is the spectator who misunderstands what he should and someday will like. The only possible contemporary comparison is with architecture, since a house has no meaning except as a habitation. The cinema is likewise a functional art. If we take another system of reference we must say of the cinema that its existence precedes its essence; even in his most adventurous extrapolations, it is this existence from which the critic must take his point of departure. As in history, and with approximately the same reservations, the verification of a change goes beyond reality and already postulates a value judgment. Those who damned the sound film at its birth were unwilling to admit precisely this, even when the sound film held the incomparable advantage over the silent film that it was replacing it.

Even if this critical pragmatism does not seem to the reader sufficiently well-founded, he must nevertheless admit that it justifies in us a certain humility and thoughtful prudence when faced with any sign of evolution in the cinema. It is in this frame of mind that we offer the explanation with which we would like to end this essay. The masterpieces to which we customarily refer as examples of true cinema—the cinema which owes nothing to the theater and literature because it is capable of discovering its own themes and language—these masterpieces are probably as admirable as they are inimitable. If the Soviet cinema no longer gives us the equivalent of *Potemkin* or Hollywood the equivalent of *Sunrise, Hallelujah, Scarface, It Happened One Night,* or even of *Stagecoach* it is not because the new generation of directors is in any way inferior to the old. As a matter of fact, they are very largely the same people. Nor is it, we believe, because economic and political factors of production have rendered their inspiration sterile. It is rather that genius and talent are relative phenomena and only develop in relation to a set of historical circumstances. It would be too simple to explain the theatrical failures of Voltaire on the grounds that he had no tragic sense; it was the age that had none. Any attempt to prolong Racinian tragedy was an incongruous undertaking in conflict with the nature of things. There is no sense in asking ourselves what the author of *Phèdre* would have written in 1740 because he whom we call Racine was not a man answering that identity, but "the-poet-who-had-written-*Phèdre*." Without *Phèdre* Racine is an anonymity, a concept of the mind. It is equally pointless in the cinema to regret that we no longer have Mack Sennett to carry on the great comic tradition. The genius of Mack Sennett was that he made his slapstick comedies at the period when this was possible. As a matter of fact, the quality of Mack Sennett productions died before he did, and certain of his pupils are still very much alive; Harold Lloyd and Buster Keaton, for example, whose rare appearances these past fifteen years have been only painful exhibitions in which nothing of the verve of yesteryear has survived. Only Chaplin has known how to span a third of a century of cinema, and this because his genius was truly exceptional. But at the price of what reincarnations, of what a total renewal of his inspiration, of his style and even of his character! We note here—the evidence is overwhelming—that strange acceleration of aesthetic continuity which characterizes the cinema. A writer may repeat himself both in matter and form over half a century. The talent of a film-maker, if he does not evolve with his art, lasts no more than five or ten years. This is why genius, less flexible and less conscious than talent, has frequent moments of extraordinary failure; for example, Stroheim, Abel Gance, Pudovkin. Certainly the causes of these profound disagreements between the artist and his art, which cruelly age genius and reduce it to nothing more than a sum of obsessions and useless megalomania, are multiple, and we are not going to analyze them here. But we would like to take up one of them which is directly related to our purpose.

Up till about 1938 the black-and-white cinema made continuous progress. At first it was a technical progress—artificial lighting, panchromatic emulsions, travelling shots, sound—and in consequence an enriching of the means of expression—close-up, montage, parallel montage, ellipsis, re-framing, and so on. Side by side with this rapid evolution of the language and in strict interdependence on it, film-makers discovered original themes to which the new art gave substance. "That is cinema!" was simply a reference to this phenomenon, which dominated the first thirty years of the film as art—that marvelous accord between a new technique and an unprecedented message. This phenomenon has taken on a great variety of forms: the star, reevaluation, the rebirth of the epic, of the *Commedia dell'Arte,* and so on. But it was directly attributable to technical progress—it was the novelty of expression which paid the price for new themes. For thirty years the history of cinematographic technique, in a broad sense, was bound up in practice with the development of the scenario. The great directors are first of all creators of form; if you wish, they are rhetoricians. This in no sense means that they supported the theory of "art for art's sake," but simply that in the dialectic of form and content, form was then the determining factor in the same way that perspective or oils turned the pictorial world upside down.

We have only to go back 10 or 15 years to observe evidence of the aging of what was the patrimony of the art of cinema. We have noted the speedy death of certain types of film, even major ones like the slapstick comedy, but the most characteristic disappearance is undoubtedly that of the star. Certain actors have always been a commercial success with the public, but this devotion has nothing in common with the socioreligious phenomenon of which Rudolph Valentino and Greta Garbo were the golden calves. It all seemed as if the area of cinematic themes had exhausted whatever it could have hoped for from technique. It was no longer enough to invent quick cutting or a new style of photography, in order to stir people's emotions. Unaware, the cinema had passed into the age of the scenario. By this we mean a reversal of the relationship between matter and form. Not that form has become a matter of indifference, quite the opposite. It had never been more rigorously determined by the content or become more necessary or a matter of greater subtlety. But all this knowledge that we have acquired operates against the intrusion of form, rendering it virtually invisible before a subject that we appreciate today for its own sake and concerning which we become more and more exacting. Like those rivers which have finally hollowed out their beds and have only the strength left to carry their waters to the sea, without adding one single grain of sand to their banks, the cinema approaches its equilibrium-profile. The days are gone when it was enough to "make cinema" in order to deserve well of the seventh art. While we wait until color or stereoscopy provisionally return its primacy to form and create a new cycle of aesthetic erosion, on the surface cinema has no longer anything to conquer. There remains for it only to irrigate its banks, to insinuate itself between the arts among which it has so swiftly carved out its valleys, subtly to invest them, to infiltrate the subsoil, in order to excavate invisible galleries. The time of resurgence of a cinema newly independent of novel and theater will return. But it may then be because novels will be written directly onto film. As it awaits the dialectic of the history of art which will restore to it this desirable and hypothetical autonomy, the cinema draws into itself the formidable resources of elaborated subjects amassed around it by neighboring arts during the course of the centuries. It will make them its own because it has need of them and we experience the desire to rediscover them by way of the cinema.

This being done, cinema will not be a substitute for them, rather will the opposite be true. The success of filmed theater helps the theater just as the adaptation of the novel serves the purpose of literature. *Hamlet* on the screen can only increase Shakespeare's public and a part of this public at least will have the taste to go and hear it on the stage. *Le Journal d'un curé de campagne,* as seen by Robert Bresson, increased Bernanos' readers tenfold. The truth is there is here no competition or substitution, rather the adding of a new dimension that the arts had gradually lost from the time of the Reformation on: namely a public.

Who will complain of that?

THEATER AND CINEMA

Part One

WHILE CRITICS often draw attention to the resemblances between the cinema and the novel, "filmed theater" still frequently passes for heresy. So long as its advocates and its prime examples were the statements and the plays of Marcel Pagnol it was reasonable enough to explain his one or two successes as flukes resulting from an unusual combination of circumstances. "Filmed theater" was bound up with recollections, in retrospect so farcical, of the *film d'art* or the boulevard hits in the "style" of Berthomieu. (Note: Unique, an incomprehensible exception at the threshold of the talking film, stands the unforgettable *Jean de la lune.*) The wartime failure of the screen adaptation of that admirable play *Le Voyageur sans baggages,* the subject of which would seem to have been suitably cinematic, apparently clinched the matter for the opponents of "filmed theater." It took a run of recent successes, from *The Little Foxes* to *Macbeth* by way of *Henry V, Hamlet,* and *Les Parents terribles,* to show that the cinema is a valid medium for a wide variety of dramatic works.

Truthfully speaking, those prejudiced against filmed theater would not have so many examples from the past to point to if the question were confined to films that were avowedly adaptations of plays. There is then some justification for looking over the history of films not according to titles but on the basis of their dramatic structure and direction.

A Brief Historical Note

While the critics were busy damning filmed theater without recourse, they were at the same time showering praise on certain forms of cinema that a closer analysis would have revealed to be the very embodiment of the art of the drama. Their vision obscured by the *film d'art* and its offspring, the customs were letting by, stamped as "pure cinema," various examples of cinematographic theater beginning with American comedy. If you look at this comedy closely you will see that it is no less "theatrical" than the adaptation of any boulevard or Broadway play. Built on comedy of dialogue and situation, most of the scenes are interiors while the editing uses the device of shot-and-reverse-shot to point up the dialogue. Here one should perhaps expound on the sociological background that made possible the brilliant development of the American comedy over a decade. The effect of this I believe would be to confirm the existence of a working relationship between theater and cinema. The cinema had, so to speak, dispensed theater from any need for prior existence. There was no such need since the authors of these plays could sell them directly to the screen. But this is a purely accidental phenomenon historically related to a combination of sociological and economic conditions now seemingly on their way out. For the past fifteen years we have seen, along with the decline of a certain type of American comedy, an increasing number of filmed Broadway comedy successes.

In the realm of psychological drama and the drama of manners, Wyler had no hesitation in taking the play by Lillian Hellman, *The*

Little Foxes, lock, stock and barrel, and bringing it to the screen virtually in its theatrical entirety. Actually there has never been any prejudice against filmed theater in the United States. But the circumstances of production in Hollywood, at least up to 1940, were not the same as in Europe. It was a matter there of a cinematographic theater restricted to certain specific genres and at least during the first decade of sound, of borrowing little from the stage. The present crisis in screen material in Hollywood has sent it looking for help more frequently to written theater. But in American comedy the theater, albeit invisible, was always potentially there.*

There is no question that we in Europe can lay no claim to an achievement comparable to the American comedy. With the exception of the special case of Marcel Pagnol, which needs a special study, boulevard comedies have failed lamentably on the screen.

Filmed theater, however, does not begin with sound. Let us go a little farther back, specifically to the time when the *film d'art* was demonstrably failing. That was the heyday of Méliès who saw the cinema as basically nothing more than a refinement of the marvels of the theater. Special effects were for him simply a further evolution of conjuring. The greater part of French and American comedians come from the music hall or from the boulevard theater. One need only look at Max Linder to see how much he owes to his theatrical experience. Like most comics of his time he plays directly

---

* In his book of reminiscences covering 50 years of cinema, entitled *The Public Is Always Right,* Adolph Zukor, creator of the star system, also tells us how the cinema in America even more than in France used its nascent awareness to plunder the theater. Realizing that the commercial future of the cinema depended on the quality of the subject matter and the prestige of the cast, Zukor bought up as many film adaptation rights as he could and enticed big names away from the theater. His salary scales, relatively high for the time, did not however always overcome the reluctance of the actors to become a part of this despised industry with its fairground flavor. Very soon, after the break with the theater, the phenomenon of the "star" peculiar to the cinema emerged, the public chose its favorites from among the famous theater names, and this elect rapidly acquired a glory with which stage fame could not be compared. Similarly, the earlier theatrical scenarios were abandoned in favor of stories adapted to the new mythology. Still, it was by copying the theater that the start had been made.

to the audience, winks at them and calls on them to witness his embarrassment, and does not shrink from asides. As for Charlie Chaplin, apart from his indebtedness to the English school of mime, it is clear that his art consists in perfecting, thanks to the cinema, his skill as a music-hall comic. Here the cinema offers more than the theater but only by going beyond it, by relieving it of its imperfections. The economics of the gag are governed by the distance between the stage and the audience and above all by the length of the laughs which spur the actor to protract his effect to the point of their extinction. The stage, then, eggs him on, forces him indeed to exaggerate. Only the screen could allow Charlie to attain mathematical perfection of situation and gesture whereby the maximum effect is obtained in the minimum of time.

When one sees again the really old slapstick films, the *Boireau* or *Onésime* series, for example, it is not only the acting which strikes one as belonging to the theater, it is also the structure of the story. The cinema makes it possible to carry a simple situation to its ultimate conclusions which on the stage would be restricted by time and space, that is, to what might be called a larval stage. What makes it possible to believe that the cinema exists to discover or create a new set of dramatic facts is its capacity to transform theatrical situations that otherwise would never have reached their maturity. In Mexico there is a kind of salamander capable of reproduction at the larval stage and which develops no further. By injecting it with hormones, scientists have brought it to maturity. In like fashion we know that the continuity of animal evolution presented us with incomprehensible gaps until biologists discovered the laws of *paidomorphosis* from which they learnt not only to place embryonic forms in the line of evolution of the species but also to recognize that certain individuals, seemingly adult, have been halted in their evolutionary development. In this sense certain types of theater are founded on dramatic situations that were congenitally atrophied prior to the appearance of the cinema. If theater is, as Jean Hytier says it is, a metaphysic of the will, what is one to think of a burlesque like *Onésime et le beau voyage*—where an obstinate determination to proceed in spite of the most ludicrous obstacles, with a not too clearly explained sort of honeymoon trip which ceases to make any sense after certain early mishaps, borders on a kind of metaphysical insanity, a delirium of the will, a cancerous regeneration of action from out of itself against all reason.

Has one even the right here to use the terminology of the psychologist and speak of will? The majority of these burlesques are an endlessly protracted expression of something that cries from within the character. They are a kind of phenomenology of obstinacy. The domestic Boireau will continue to do the housework till the house collapses in ruins. Onésime, the migratory spouse, will continue on his honeymoon trip to the point of embarking for the horizon in his wicker trunk. The action here no longer calls for plot, episodes, repercussions, misunderstandings, or sudden reversals. It unfolds implacably to the point at which it destroys itself. It proceeds unswervingly towards a kind of rudimentary catharsis of catastrophe like a small child recklessly inflating a rubber balloon to the point where it explodes in his face—to our relief and possibly to his.

For the rest, when one examines the history of the characters, situations, and routines of classical farce it is impossible to avoid the conclusion that slapstick cinema gave it a sudden and dazzling rebirth. The "flesh and blood farce," on its way out since the seventeenth century, survived, highly specialized and transformed, only in the circus and in certain kinds of music hall. That is to say precisely in these places where the Hollywood producers of slapstick films went for their actors. The routines of this genre combined with the resources of the cinema added widely to their technical repertory. It made possible a Max Linder, a Buster Keaton, a Laurel and Hardy, a Chaplin. Between 1903 and 1920 it reached a peak unique in its history. I am referring to the tradition of farce as it has been perpetuated since the days of Plautus and Terence and even including the *Commedia dell'Arte* with its special themes and techniques. Let me take just one example. The "vat routine" turns up spontaneously in an old Max Linder around 1912 or 1913 in which we see the sprightly Don Juan seducer of the dyer's wife forced to take a header into a vat full of dye to escape the vengeance of the cheated husband. In a case like this there is no question of imitation, or of influence or of a remembered routine, just the spontaneous linking up of a genre with its tradition.

The Text! The Text!

It is clear from these few recollections from the past that the relations between theater and cinema are much older and closer than is generally thought to be the case and that they are certainly not limited to what is generally and deprecatingly called "filmed theater." We have also seen that the influence, as unconscious as it was unavowed, of the repertory and traditions of theater has been very marked on that class of film considered purely and specifically cinematic.

But the problem of the adaptation of a play as we generally use the term is something different again. We must begin, before going any further, by distinguishing between theatrical reality and dramatic reality.

Drama is the soul of the theater but this soul sometimes inhabits other bodies. A sonnet, a fable of La Fontaine, a novel, a film can owe their effectiveness to what Henri Gouhier calls *"the dramatic categories."* From this point of view it is useless to claim autonomy for the theater. Either that, or we must show it to be something negative. That is to say a play cannot not be dramatic while a novel is free to be dramatic or not. *Of Mice and Men* is simultaneously a novel and a model tragedy. On the other hand, it would be very hard to adapt *Swann's Way* for the theater. One would not praise a play for its novel-like qualities yet one may very well congratulate a novelist for being able to structure an action.

Nevertheless, if we insist that the dramatic is exclusive to theater, we must concede its immense influence and also that the cinema is the least likely of the arts to escape this influence. At this rate, half of literature and three quarters of the existing films are branches of theater. It is equally true that this is not the way to state the problem. The problem only came alive by virtue of the incarnation of the theatrical work not in the actor but in the text.

Phèdre was written to be played but it also exists as a work and as a tragedy for the student as he labors the year round at his classics. "Armchair theater," having only imagination to rely on, is lacking as theater, but it is nevertheless still theater. On the contrary *Cyrano de Bergerac* or *Le Voyageur sans baggages* as filmed are *not,* in spite of the text and of a generous dose of spectacle into the bargain.

If it were permissible to take just one single action from *Phèdre,* to reconstruct it according to the requirements of the novel or of cinematic dialogue, we would find ourselves back with our earlier hypothesis, namely of the theatrical reduced to the dramatic. Now while, metaphysically speaking, there is nothing to prevent one from doing this, there are a number of historical and purely practical arguments against it. The simplest of them is a salutary fear of the ridiculous, while the most forceful is our modern attitude towards a work of art which demands respect for the text and for the rights of authorship, and which is morally binding even after the author's death. In other words, only Racine has the right to make an adaptation of *Phèdre.* But here, over and above the fact that even so there is no guarantee that it would be any good (Anouilh himself adapted *Le Voyageur sans baggages*) there is also another fact to consider. Racine happens to be dead.

Some will hold that the situation is not the same during an author's lifetime, since he can himself revise his work and remodel his material. André Gide did this recently although in an opposite direction, namely from novel to screen with *Les Caves du Vatican.* At least he can keep an eye on the result and guarantee the adaptation. A closer examination however shows that this is a matter rather of jurisdiction than of aesthetics. In the first place talent, and still less genius, are not to be found everywhere, and nothing can guarantee that the original and the adaptation will be of the same standard even if they are the work of the same author. Furthermore, the usual reason for wanting to make a film out of a contemporary play is its commercial success in the theater. In the course of its successful run, the text, as tried out, has become crystallized so to speak as to its essentials and it is this text that the film audience will be looking for. So here we are, by way of a more or less honorable detour, back at our respect for the written text.

Finally it may be argued that the greater the dramatic quality of a work the more difficult it is to separate off the dramatic from the theatrical element, a synthesis of the two having been achieved in the text. It is significant that while novels are often dramatized, a novel is rarely made from a play. It is as if the theater stood at the end of an irreversible process of aesthetic refinement.

Strictly speaking one could make a play out of *Madame Bovary* or *The Brothers Karamazov*. But had the plays come first it would be impossible to derive from them the novels as we know them. In other words, when the drama is so much a part of the novel that it cannot be taken from it, reciprocally the novel can only be the result of a process of induction which in the arts means purely and simply a new creation. Compared with the play, the novel is only one of the many possible syntheses derivable from the simple dramatic element.

I am comparing for the moment novel and theater but there is every reason to suppose that the argument applies with greater force to the cinema. For we have one of two things to choose from. The film is either the photographed play, text and all, in which case we have our famous "filmed theater." Or the play is adapted to the requirements of the cinema and we are back with the composite that we spoke of above and it is a question of a new work. Jean Renoir drew his inspiration for *Boudu sauvé des eaux* from the play by René Fauchois but he made a superior thing of it, which in all probability eclipsed the original.* This is, incidentally, an exception that definitely proves the rule.

However one approaches it, a play whether classic or modern is unassailably protected by its text. There is no way of adapting the text without disposing of it and substituting something else, which may be better but is not the play. This is a practice, for that matter, restricted of necessity to second-class authors or to those still living, since the masterpieces that time has hallowed demand, as a postulate, that we respect their texts.

The experience of the last ten years bears this out. If the problem of filmed theater has taken on a new lease of aesthetic life it is thanks to films like *Hamlet, Henry V,* and *Macbeth* among the classics, and among contemporary works films like *The Little Foxes* by Lillian Hellman and Wyler, *Les Parents terribles, Occupe-toi d'Amélie, Rope.* Jean Cocteau had written an adaptation of *Les Parents terribles* prior to the war. When he took up the project again in 1946 he decided to go back to the original text. As we shall see, a little later he also virtually preserved the original stage settings. Whether it has been in the United States, England, or France, both with the classics and the contemporary plays, the evolution of filmed theater has been the same. It has been characterized by an increasingly exacting demand for fidelity to the text as originally written. It is as if all the various experiments of the sound film had converged on this point.

Previously the first concern of a film-maker was to disguise the theatrical origins of his model, to adapt it and to dissolve it in cinema. Not only does he seem to have abandoned this attitude, he makes a point of emphasizing its theatrical character. It could not be otherwise from the moment we preserve the essentials of the text. Conceived with a view to the potentialities of the theater, these are already embodied in the text. The text determines the mode and style of the production; it is already potentially the the-

---

* He took no less a liberty with *La Carosse du S. Sacrement* by Merimée.

ater. There is no way at one and the same time of being faithful to it and of turning it aside from the direction it was supposed to go.

Hide That Theater Which I Cannot Abide!

We shall find a confirmation of this in an example borrowed from classical theater. It is a film that may still, perhaps, be creating havoc in French schools and lycées and which pretends to offer a method of teaching literature through cinema. I refer to *Le Médecin malgré lui*. It was brought to the screen, with the help of a doubtlessly well-intentioned teacher, by a director whose name we will not disclose. This film has a dossier, as laudatory as it is depressing, from professors and headmasters of lycées who are delighted by its fine qualities. In reality it is an unbelievable collection of all the faults guaranteed to make an end of film and theater alike, to say nothing of Molière himself. The first scene, with the bundles of wood, set in a real forest, opens with an interminable travelling shot through the underbrush, destined obviously to allow us to enjoy the effects of sunlight on the underside of the branches before showing us two clownlike characters who are presumably gathering mushrooms and whose stage costumes, in this setting, look like nothing so much as grotesque disguises. Real settings are used as much as possible throughout the film. The arrival of Sganarelle for a consultation is seized upon as an opportunity to show us a small country manor house of the seventeenth century. And what of the editing? In the first scene it moves from medium full-shot to full-shot, cross cutting with each piece of dialogue. One has the feeling that if the text, much against the director's will, had not dictated the length of film, he would have presented the flow of dialogue in that speeded-up form of editing we associate with Abel Gance. Such as it is, the editing sees to it that the students, through the use of shot-and-reverse-shot in close-up, miss nothing of the

miming of the cast from the Comédie Française, which unquestionably takes us back to the heyday of the *film d'art.*

If by cinema we understand liberty of action in regard to space,
and freedom to choose your angle of approach to the action, then
filming a play should give the setting a breadth and reality un-
attainable on the stage. It would also free the spectator from his
seat and by varying the shots give an added quality to the acting.

Faced with productions of this kind, one must agree that every
argument against filmed theater is a valid one. But the problem is
not with the production at all. What was actually done was to inject
the power of "cinema" into the theater. The original drama and the
text even more so have been turned out of house and home, so to
speak. The duration of the action on the stage and on screen are
obviously not the same. The dramatic primacy of the word is
thrown off center by the additional dramatization that the camera
gives to the setting. Finally and above all, a certain artificiality, an
exaggerated transformation of the decor, is totally incompatible
with that realism which is of the essence of the cinema. The text of
Molière only takes on meaning in a forest of painted canvas and the
same is true of the acting. The footlights are not the autumn sun. If
it comes to that, the scene of the bundles of wood could be played
in front of a curtain. It no longer calls for the foot of a tree.

This failure is a good example of what may be considered the
major heresy of filmed theater, namely the urge "to make cinema."
By and large this is responsible for the majority of adaptations of
successful plays. If the action is supposed to take place on the Côte
d'Azur, the lovers, instead of chatting in a nook of a bar, will be
kissing at the wheel of an American car as they drive along the
Corniche against a back projection showing the rocks of the Cap
d'Antibes. As for editing, the contracts of Raimu and Fernandel
being the same will assure us of a reasonably equal number of close-
ups favoring now one and now the other.

Besides, the preconceptions of the public in these matters serve
to confirm those of the film-makers. People in general do not give

much thought to the cinema. For them it means vast decor, exteriors, and plenty of action. If they are not given at least a minimum of what they call cinema, they feel cheated. The cinema must be more lavish than the theater. Every actor must be a somebody and any hint of poverty or meanness in the everyday surrounding contributes, so they say, to a flop. Obviously then, a director or a producer who is willing to challenge the public prejudice in these matters needs courage. Especially if they do not have too much faith in what they are doing. The heresy of filmed theater is rooted in an ambivalent complex that cinema has about the theater. It is an inferiority complex in the presence of an older and more literary art, for which the cinema proceeds to overcompensate by the "superiority" of its technique—which in turn is mistaken for an aesthetic superiority.

Canned or Supertheater?

Would you like to see these errors disproved? Two successful films like *Henry V* and *Les Parents terribles* will do the job perfectly.

When the director of *Le Médecin malgré lui* opened on a travelling shot in the forest, it was with the naive and perhaps unconscious hope that it would help us swallow the unfortunate scene with the bundles of wood like a sugar-coated pill. He tried to give us a little environment of reality, to give us a ladder onto the stage. His awkward tricks had, unfortunately, the opposite effect. They underlined the unreality of both the characters and the text.

Now let us see how Laurence Olivier succeeded in resolving the dialectic between cinematic realism and theatrical convention. His film also begins with a travelling shot, but in this case its purpose is to plunge us into the theater, the courtyard of an Elizabethan inn. He is not pretending to make us forget the conventions of the theater. On the contrary he affirms them. It is not with the play

Henry V that the film is immediately and directly concerned, but with a performance of *Henry V*. This we know from the fact that the performance here given is not supposed to be an actual one, as when the play is given in the theater. It is supposed to be taking place in Shakespeare's day and we are even shown the audience and the backstage areas. There is no mistake about it, the act of faith usually required of a spectator as the curtain rises is not needed here for the enjoyment of the spectacle. We are not in the play, we are in an historical film about the Elizabethan theater, that is to say, we are present at a film of a kind that is widely accepted and to which we are quite used. Our enjoyment of the play however is not of the kind we would get from an historical documentary. It is in fact the pleasure to be derived from a Shakespearean performance. In other words the aesthetic strategy of Laurence Olivier was a trick to escape from the "miracle of the curtain," that is, from the need for the usual suspension of disbelief.

In making his film out of a play by showing us, from the opening, by a cinematic device that we are concerned here with theatrical style and conventions instead of trying to hide them, he relieved realism of that which makes it the foe of theatrical illusion. Once assured of a psychological hold on the complicity of the spectator, Olivier could then perfectly well allow himself the switch in pictorial style to the battle of Agincourt. Shakespeare invited it by his deliberate appeal to the imagination of the spectator; here again Olivier had a perfect excuse. This recourse to the cinematic, difficult to justify if the film was just a reproduction of the play, finds its justification in the play itself. Naturally he still had to honor his promise and we know that he did this. Let us simply remark here that the color, which may eventually come to seem an essentially unrealistic element, helps to justify the transition to the realm of the imaginary and once there to make it possible to accept a continuity which passes from miniatures to a realistic reconstruction of the battle of Agincourt. Never for one moment is *Henry V* really "filmed theater." The film exists so to speak side by side with the theatrical presentation, in front of and behind the stage. Both Shakespeare and the theater however are truly its prisoners, hemmed in on all sides by cinema.

The boulevard theater of today does not appear to make quite such obvious use of the conventions of theater. The *"Théâtre Libre"* and the theories of Antoine might even lead one to believe in the existence at one time of a "realist" theater, a kind of pre-cinema.* This is an illusion that no longer fools anybody. If there is such a thing, it is again only something that relates to a system of less obvious conventions, less explicit but just as absolute. There is no such thing as a "slice of life" in the theater. In any case, the mere fact that it is exposed to view on the stage removes it from everyday existence and turns it into something seen as it were in a shop window. It is in a measure part of the natural order but it is profoundly modified by the conditions under which we observe it.

Antoine might decorate the stage with real joints of meat but, unlike the cinema, he could not show a whole flock of sheep passing by. If he wanted to plant a tree on the stage he had first to uproot it and in any case he had to give up any idea of showing the entire

---

* A comment here might not come amiss. We must first of all recognize that melodrama and drama stirred up a realist revolution at the very core of the theater: the ideal stendhalian spectator fires a revolver at the traitor in the play (Orson Welles was later to do the opposite on Broadway and turn a machinegun on the orchestra stalls). A hundred years later, Antoine will stage a realist text by way of realist *mise-en-scène*. If Antoine subsequently made films it was not just a coincidence. The fact is that if one goes back a little into history, one must agree that an elaborate attempt at "theater-cinema" had already preceded "cinema-theater." Dumas *fils* and Antoine were the precursors of Marcel Pagnol. It could very well be that the renaissance in theater spurred by Antoine was greatly aided by the existence of cinema, which had taken upon its own head the heresy of realism and limited the theories of Antoine to a reasonable and effective reaction against symbolism. The choice that the Vieux Colombier had made during the revolution of the Théâtre Libre (leaving realism to the Grand Guignol), reasserting the value of stage conventions, might not have been possible without the competition of the cinema. It was a perfect example of competition which, whatever happens, has finally laughed dramatic realism out of court. Nobody can pretend today that even the most bourgeois of boulevard dramas is without its full share of theatrical conventions.

forest. So really his tree still derives from the Elizabethan placard which in the end is only a signpost. If we bear these undoubted truths in mind we will then admit that the filming of a melodrama like *Les Parents terribles* presents problems very little different from filming a classic play. What we here call realism does not at all place the play on the same footing as the cinema. It does not do away with the footlights. To put it simply, the system of conventions that govern the production and hence the text are, so to speak, at the initial level. The conventions of tragedy with their procession of odd-looking properties and their alexandrines are but masks and cothurni that confirm and emphasize the basic convention which is theater.

Cocteau was well aware of this when he filmed his *Parents terribles*. Again, since his play was markedly realist, Cocteau the film-maker understood that he must add nothing to the setting, that the role of the cinema was not to multiply but to intensify . . . if the room of the play became an apartment in the film, thanks to the screen and to the camera it would feel even more cramped than the room on the stage. What it was essential to bring out was a sense of people being shut in and living in close proximity. A single ray of sunlight, any other than electric light, would have destroyed that delicately balanced and inescapable coexistence. The crowded coach too may travel to the other end of Paris, to Madeleine's house. We leave it at the door of one apartment to discover it at the door of the other. We do not have here the example of the classical editing short-cut but a positive part of the direction, which the cinema did not impose on Cocteau and who thereby went beyond the expressive possibilities of the theater. The latter, being restricted, cannot therefore produce the same effect. A hundred examples could be adduced to confirm the respect of the camera for the stage setting, its concern being only to increase the effectiveness of the settings and never to attempt to interfere with their relation to the characters of the play. All the annoyances of theater are not so easily disposed of. Having to show each room in succession and meanwhile to lower the curtain is without doubt a pointless imposition. Thanks to its mobility, it is the camera that is responsible for the real unity of time and place. The theater needed the cinema before it could freely express what it had to say and *Les Parents terribles* could be shown to be a tragedy of an apartment in which a door left ajar could take on more significance than a monologue on a bed. Cocteau never lets his work down, his respect for what are the essential requirements being the greater in proportion as he is able to separate them from those happenings which are not essential. The function of the cinema is to reveal, to bring to light certain details that the stage would have left untreated.

The problem of the decor having been solved, the most difficult one still remained, namely the editing. Here Cocteau gave proof of his ingenious imagination. The notion of "shot" is finally disposed of. There remains henceforth only the question of framing the fleeting crystallization of a reality of whose environing presence one is ceaselessly aware. Cocteau likes to tell how he thought his film through in 16mm. "Thought it through" is right. He would have been hard put to direct it in anything less than 35mm. What is important here is for the spectator to have a feeling of being totally present at what is going on, not as in Welles' pictures (or in Renoir's) through depth of focus but by virtue of a diabolic speed of vision which seems for the first time to be wedded here to the pure rhythm of attention. Undoubtedly all good editing takes this into consideration. The traditional device of shot-reverse-shot divides up the dialogue according to an elementary syntax of interest. The close-up of a telephone that rings at a pathetic moment is the equivalent of a concentration of attention. It seems to us however that normal editing is a compromise between three ways of possibly analyzing reality.

(1) *A purely logical and descriptive analysis* (the weapon used in the crime lying beside the corpse). (2) *A psychological analysis* from within the film, namely one that fits the point of view of one of the protagonists in a given situation. An example of this would

be the glass of milk that may possibly be poisoned which Ingrid Bergman has to drink in *Notorious,* or the ring on the finger of Theresa Wright in *The Shadow of a Doubt.* (3) *Finally, a psychological analysis from the point of view of spectator interest,* either a spontaneous interest or one provoked by the director thanks precisely to this analysis. An example of this would be the handle of a door turning unseen by the criminal who thinks he is alone. ("Look out," the children used to shout to the Guignol whom the policeman is about to surprise.)

These three points of view which combined together constitute the synthesis of cinematographic events in most films are felt to be unique. Actually they imply at once a psychological heterogeneity and a material discontinuity. They are basically the same as those peddled by the traditional novelist—which, as we know, brought down the wrath of J.-P. Sartre on the head of François Mauriac. The importance of depth of focus and the fixed camera in the films of Orson Welles and William Wyler springs from a reluctance to fragment things arbitrarily and a desire instead to show an image that is uniformly understandable and that compels the spectator to make his own choice.

Although he remains faithful to the classic pattern of cutting— his film includes a fair number of shots above medium—Cocteau gives it a special significance by using, practically exclusively, shots from category number three above. Logical and descriptive analysis together with points of view of the actor are virtually eliminated. There remain those of the witness. The subjective camera finally becomes a reality but in an opposite sense, that is to say not as in *The Lady in the Lake,* thanks to a puerile kind of identification of the spectator and the character by means of a camera trick but, on the contrary, through the pitiless gaze of an invisible witness. The camera is at last a spectator and nothing else. The drama is once more a spectacle. It was indeed Cocteau who said that cinema is an event seen through a keyhole. The impression we get here from the keyhole is of an invasion of privacy, the quasi-obscenity of "viewing." Let us take a highly significant example of this position of "exteriority." It is one of the final shots of the picture when Yvonne de Bray, poisoned, is withdrawing backwards into her own room, her eyes on the busy group around the happy Madeleine. The camera pulls back to accompany her. But the movement of the camera, no matter how great the temptation, is never confused with the subjective viewpoint of "Sophie." The shock of the travelling shot would be certainly more violent if we were in the position of the actress and were looking with her eyes. But Cocteau carefully avoided this false move. He keeps Yvonne de Bray "as bait" and pulls back, retreating a little, behind her. The purpose of the shot is to show not that she is looking, not even her gaze, it is to *see her actually looking.* It is done doubtless over her shoulder as is the privilege of cinema—one which Cocteau hastens to restore to the theater.

He thus returned to the principle of audience-stage relations. While the cinema allowed him to seize upon the drama from many angles, he deliberately chose to adopt the viewpoint of the spectator, the one denominator common to stage and screen.

So Cocteau maintains the essentially theatrical character of his play. Instead of trying like so many others to dissolve it in cinema, on the contrary he uses the resources of the camera to point up, to underline, to confirm the structure of the scenes and their psychological corollaries. The specific help given here by the cinema can only be described as an added measure of the theatrical.

As a result he joins ranks with Laurence Olivier, Orson Welles, Wyler, and Dudley Nichols. This is borne out by an analysis of *Macbeth, Hamlet, The Little Foxes,* and *Mourning Becomes Electra,* to say nothing of a film like *Occupe-toi d'Amélie* where Claude Autant-Lara does with vaudeville something comparable to what Olivier does with *Henry V.* All these very characteristic successes of the past fifteen years illustrate a paradox. One is no longer adapting a subject. One is staging a play by means of cinema. The problem

What Is Cinema?

of "canned" theater, whether it is a naive or an impudent question, has certainly taken on a new lease of life as a result of these recent successes. We have tried to see how it happened. Now, more ambitious than ever, will we be able to find out why?

THEATER AND CINEMA

Part Two

THE LEITMOTIV of those who despise filmed theater, their final and apparently insuperable argument, continues to be the unparalleled pleasure that accompanies the presence of the actor. "What is specific to theater," writes Henri Gouhier, in *The Essence of Theater,* "is the impossibility of separating off action and actor." Elsewhere he says "the stage welcomes every illusion except that of presence; the actor is there in disguise, with the soul and voice of another, but he is nevertheless there and by the same token space calls out for him and for the solidity of his presence. On the other hand and inversely, the cinema accommodates every form of reality save one —the physical presence of the actor." If it is here that the essence of theater lies then undoubtedly the cinema can in no way pretend to any parallel with it. If the writing, the style, and the dramatic structure are, as they should be, rigorously conceived as the receptacle for the soul and being of the flesh-and-blood actor, any attempt to substitute the shadow and reflection of a man on the screen for the man himself is a completely vain enterprise. There is no answer to this argument. The successes of Laurence Olivier, of Welles, or of Cocteau can only be challenged—here you need to be in bad faith—or considered inexplicable. They are a challenge both to critics and philosophers. Alternatively one can only explain them by casting doubts on that commonplace of theatrical criticism "the irreplacable presence of the actor."

The Concept of Presence

At this point certain comments seem called for concerning the concept of "presence," since it would appear that it is this concept, as understood prior to the appearance of photography, that the cinema challenges.

Can the photographic image, especially the cinematographic image, be likened to other images and in common with them be regarded as having an existence distinct from the object? Presence, naturally, is defined in terms of time and space. "To be in the presence of someone" is to recognize him as existing contemporaneously with us and to note that he comes within the actual range of our senses—in the case of cinema of our sight and in radio of our hearing. Before the arrival of photography and later of cinema, the plastic arts (especially portraiture) were the only intermediaries between actual physical presence and absence. Their justification was their resemblance which stirs the imagination and helps the memory. But photography is something else again. In no sense is it the image of an object or person, more correctly it is its tracing. Its automatic genesis distinguishes it radically from the other techniques of reproduction. The photograph proceeds by means of the lens to the taking of a veritable luminous impression in light—to a mold. As such it carries with it more than mere resemblance, namely a kind of identity—the card we call by that name being only conceivable in an age of photography. But photography is a feeble technique in the sense that its instantaneity compels it to capture time only piecemeal. The cinema does something strangely paradoxical. It makes a molding of the object as it exists in time and, furthermore, makes an imprint of the duration of the object.

The nineteenth century with its objective techniques of visual and sound reproduction gave birth to a new category of images, the relation of which to the reality from which they proceed requires very strict definition. Even apart from the fact that the resulting aesthetic problems cannot be satisfactorily raised without this introductory philosophical inquiry, it would not be sound to treat the old aesthetic questions as if the categories with which they deal had in no way been modified by the appearance of completely new phenomena. Common sense—perhaps the best philosophical guide in this case—has clearly understood this and has invented an expression for the presence of an actor, by adding to the placards announcing his appearance the phrase "in flesh and blood." This means that for the man in the street the word "presence," today, can be ambiguous, and thus an apparent redundancy is not out of place in this age of cinema. Hence it is no longer as certain as it was that there is no middle stage between presence and absence. It is likewise at the ontological level that the effectiveness of the cinema has its source. It is false to say that the screen is incapable of putting us "in the presence of" the actor. It does so in the same way as a mirror—one must agree that the mirror relays the presence of the person reflected in it—but it is a mirror with a delayed reflection, the tin foil of which retains the image.* It is true that in the

---

* Television naturally adds a new variant to the "pseudopresences" resulting from the scientific techniques for reproduction created by photography. On the little screen during live television the actor is actually present in space and time. But the reciprocal actor-spectator relationship is incomplete in one direction. The spectator sees without being seen. There is no return flow. Televised theater, therefore, seems to share something both of theater and of cinema: of theater because the actor is present to the viewer, of cinema because the spectator is not present to the actor. Nevertheless, this state of not being present is not truly an absence. The television actor has a sense of the millions of ears and eyes virtually present and represented by the electronic camera. This abstract presence is most noticeable when the actor fluffs his

theater Molière can die on the stage and that we have the privilege of living in the biographical time of the actor. In the film about Manolete however we are present at the actual death of the famous matador and while our emotion may not be as deep as if we were actually present in the arena at that historic moment, its nature is the same. What we lose by way of direct witness do we not recapture thanks to the artificial proximity provided by photographic enlargement? Everything takes place as if in the time-space perimeter which is the definition of presence. The cinema offers us effectively only a measure of duration, reduced but not to zero, while the increase in the space factor reestablishes the equilibrium of the psychological equation.

Opposition and Identification

An honest appraisal of the respective pleasures derived from theater and cinema, at least as to what is less intellectual and more direct about them, forces us to admit that the delight we experience at the end of a play has a more uplifting, a nobler, one might perhaps say a more moral, effect than the satisfaction which follows a good film. We seem to come away with a better conscience. In a certain sense it is as if for the man in the audience all theater is "Corneillian." From this point of view one could say that in the best films something is missing. It is as if a certain inevitable lowering of the voltage, some mysterious aesthetic short circuit, deprived us in the cinema of a certain tension which is a definite part of theater. No matter how slight this difference it undoubtedly exists, even between the worst charity production in the theater and the most brilliant of Olivier's film adaptations. There is nothing banal about

---

lines. Painful enough in the theater, it is intolerable on television since the spectator who can do nothing to help him is aware of the unnatural solitude of the actor. In the theater in similar circumstances a sort of understanding exists with the audience, which is a help to an actor in trouble. This kind of reciprocal relationship is impossible on television.

this observation and the survival of the theater after fifty years of cinema, and the prophecies of Marcel Pagnol, is practical proof enough. At the source of the disenchantment which follows the film one could doubtless detect a process of depersonalization of the spectator. As Rosenkrantz wrote in 1937, in *Esprit,* in an article profoundly original for its period, "The characters on the screen are quite naturally objects of identification, while those on the stage are, rather, objects of mental opposition because their real presence gives them an objective reality and to transpose them into beings in an imaginary world the will of the spectator has to intervene actively, that is to say, to will to transform their physical reality into an abstraction. This abstraction being the result of a process of the intelligence that we can only ask of a person who is fully conscious." A member of a film audience tends to identify himself with the film's hero by a psychological process, the result of which is to turn the audience into a "mass" and to render emotion uniform. Just as in algebra if two numbers equal a third, then they are equal to one another, so here we can say, if two individuals identify themselves with a third, they identify themselves with one another. Let us compare chorus girls on the stage and on the screen. On the screen they satisfy an unconscious sexual desire and when the hero joins them he satisfies the desire of the spectator in the proportion to which the latter has identified himself with the hero. On the stage the girls excite the onlooker as they would in real life. The result is that there is no identification with the hero. He becomes instead an object of jealousy and envy. In other words, Tarzan is only possible on the screen. The cinema calms the spectator, the theater excites him. Even when it appeals to the lowest instincts, the theater up to a certain point stands in the way of the creation of a mass mentality.* It stands in the way of any collective representation in the psychological sense, since theater calls for an active individual consciousness while the film requires only a passive adhesion.

---

* Crowd and solitude are not antinomies: the audience in a movie house is made up of solitary individuals. Crowd should be taken here to mean the opposite of an organic community freely assembled.

These views shed a new light on the problem of the actor. They transfer him from the ontological to the psychological level. It is to the extent to which the cinema encourages identification with the hero that it conflicts with the theater. Put this way the problem is no longer basically insoluble, for it is a fact that the cinema has at its disposal means which favor a passive position or on the other hand, means which to a greater or lesser degree stimulate the consciousness of the spectator. Inversely the theater can find ways of lessening the psychological tension between spectator and actor. Thus theater and cinema will no longer be separated off by an unbridgeable aesthetic moat, they would simply tend to give rise to two attitudes of mind over which the director maintains a wide control.

Examined at close quarters, the pleasure derived from the theater not only differs from that of the cinema but also from that of the novel. The reader of a novel, physically alone like the man in the dark movie house, identifies himself with the character.* That is why after reading for a long while he also feels the same intoxication of an illusory intimacy with the hero. Incontestably, there is in the pleasure derived from cinema and novel a self-satisfaction, a concession to solitude, a sort of betrayal of action by a refusal of social responsibility.

The analysis of this phenomenon might indeed be undertaken from a psychoanalytic point of view. It is not significant that the psychiatrists took the term catharsis from Aristotle? Modern pedagogic research on psychodrama seems to have provided fruitful insights into the cathartic process of theater. The ambiguity existing in the child's mind between play and reality is used to get him to free himself by way of improvised theater from the repressions from which he suffers. This technique amounts to creating a kind of vague theater in which the play is of a serious nature and the actor is his own audience. The action that develops on these

---

* Cf. Cl. E. Magny, *L'Age du roman américain,* ed. Du Seuil.

occasions is not one that is divided off by footlights, which are undoubtedly the architectural symbol of the censor that separates us from the stage. We delegate Oedipus to act in our guise and place him on the other side of a wall of fire—that fiery frontier between fantasy and reality which gives rein to Dionysiac monsters while protecting us from them.* These sacred beasts will not cross this barrier of light beyond which they seem out of place and even sacrilegious—witness the disturbing atmosphere of awe which surrounds an actor still made up, like a phosphorescent light, when we visit him in his dressing room. There is no point to the argument that the theater did not always have footlights. These are only a symbol and there were others before them from the cothurnus and mask onwards. In the seventeenth century the fact that young nobles sat up on the stage is no denial of the role of the footlights, on the contrary, it confirms it, by way of a privileged violation so to speak, just as when today Orson Welles scatters actors around the auditorium to fire on the audience with revolvers. He does not do away with the footlights, he just crosses them. The rules of the game are also made to be broken. One expects some players to cheat.† With regard to the objection based on presence and on that alone, the theater and the cinema are not basically in conflict. What is really in dispute are two psychological modalities of a per-

---

* Cf. P. A. Touchard, *Dionysos,* ed. Du Seuil.

† Here is a final example proving that presence does not constitute theater except in so far as it is a matter of a performance. Everyone either at his own or someone else's expense has known the embarrassment of being watched without knowing it or in spite of knowing it. Lovers who kiss on public benches offer a spectacle to the passerby, but they do not care. My concierge who has a feeling for the *mot juste* says, when she sees them, that it is like being at the movies. Each of us has sometimes found himself forced to his annoyance to do something absurd before other people. On those occasions we experience a sense of angry shame which is the very opposite of theatrical exhibitionism. Someone who looks through a keyhole is not at the theater; Cocteau has rightly demonstrated in *Le sang d'un poète* that he was already at the cinema. And nevertheless there are such things as "shows," when the protagonists are present to us in flesh and blood but one of the two parties is ignorant of the fact or goes through with it reluctantly. This is not "play" in the theatrical sense.

formance. The theater is indeed based on the reciprocal awareness of the presence of audience and actor, but only as related to a performance. The theater acts on us by virtue of our participation in a theatrical action across the footlights and as it were under the protection of their censorship. The opposite is true in the cinema. Alone, hidden in a dark room, we watch through half-open blinds a spectacle that is unaware of our existence and which is part of the universe. There is nothing to prevent us from identifying ourselves in imagination with the moving world before us, which becomes *the* world. It is no longer on the phenomenon of the actor as a person physically present that we should concentrate our analysis, but rather on the ensemble of conditions that constitute the theatrical play and deprive the spectator of active participation. We shall see that it is much less a question of actor and presence than of man and his relation to the decor.

Behind the Decor

The human being is all-important in the theater. The drama on the screen can exist without actors. A banging door, a leaf in the wind, waves beating on the shore can heighten the dramatic effect. Some film masterpieces use man only as an accessory, like an extra, or in counterpoint to nature which is the true leading character. Even when, as in *Nanook* and *Man of Aran,* the subject is man's struggle with nature, it cannot be compared to a theatrical action. The mainspring of the action is not in man but nature. As Jean-Paul Sartre, I think it was, said, in the theater the drama proceeds from the actor, in the cinema it goes from the decor to man. This reversal of the dramatic flow is of decisive importance. It is bound up with the very essence of the *mise-en-scène*. One must see here one of the consequences of photographic realism. Obviously, if the cinema makes use of nature it is because it is able to. The camera puts at the disposal of the director all the resources of the telescope and the microscope. The last strand of a rope about to snap or an entire army making an assault on a hill are within our reach. Dramatic causes and effects have no longer any material limits to the eye of the camera. Drama is freed by the camera from all contingencies of time and space. But this freeing of tangible dramatic powers is still only a secondary aesthetic cause, and does not basically explain the reversal of value between the actor and the decor. For sometimes it actually happens that the cinema deliberately deprives itself of the use of setting and of exterior nature—we have already seen a perfect instance of this in *Les Parents terribles*—while the theater in contrast uses a complex machinery to give a feeling of ubiquity to the audience. Is *La Passion de Jeanne d'Arc* by Carl Dreyer, shot entirely in close-up, in the virtually invisible and in fact theatrical settings by Jean Hugo, less cinematic than *Stagecoach?* It seems to me that quantity has nothing to do with it, nor the resemblance to certain theater techniques. The ideas of an art director for a room in *Les Dames aux camélias* would not noticeably differ whether for a film or a play. It's true that on the screen you would doubtless have some close-ups of the blood-stained handkerchief, but a skillful stage production would also know how to make some play with the cough and the handkerchief. All the close-ups in *Les Parents terribles* are taken directly from the theater where our attention would spontaneously isolate them. If film direction only differed from theater direction because it allows us a closer view of the scenery and makes a more reasonable use of it, there would really be no reason to continue with the theater and Pagnol would be a true prophet. For it is obvious that the few square yards of the decor of Vilar's *La Danse de la mort* contributed as much to the drama as the island on which Marcel Cravene shot his excellent film. The fact is that the problem lies not in the decor itself but in

103

its nature and function. We must therefore throw some light on an essentially theatrical notion, that of the dramatic place.

There can be no theater without architecture, whether it be the cathedral square, the arena of Nîmes, the palace of the Popes, the trestle stage on a fairground, the semicircle of the theater of Vicenza that looks as if it were decorated by Bérard in a delirium, or the rococo amphitheaters of the boulevard houses. Whether as a performance or a celebration, theater of its very essence must not be confused with nature under penalty of being absorbed by her and ceasing to be. Founded on the reciprocal awareness of those taking part and present to one another, it must be in contrast to the rest of the world in the same way that play and reality are opposed, or concern and indifference, or liturgy and the common use of things. Costume, mask, or make-up, the style of the language, the footlights, all contribute to this distinction, but the clearest sign of all is the stage, the architecture of which has varied from time to time without ever ceasing to mark out a privileged spot actually or virtually distinct from nature. It is precisely in virtue of this *locus dramaticus* that decor exists. It serves in greater or less degree to set the place apart, to specify. Whatever it is, the decor constitutes the walls of this three-sided box opening onto the auditorium, which we call the stage. These false perspectives, these façades, these arbors, have another side which is cloth and nails and wood. Everyone knows that when the actor "retires to his apartment" from the yard or from the garden, he is actually going to his dressing room to take off his make-up. These few square feet of light and illusion are surrounded by machinery and flanked by wings, the hidden labyrinths of which do not interfere one bit with the pleasure of the spectator who is playing the game of theater. Because it is only part of the architecture of the stage, the decor of the theater is thus an area materially enclosed, limited, circumscribed, the only discoveries of which are those of our collusive imagination.

Its appearances are turned inward facing the public and the

footlights. It exists by virtue of its reverse side and its absence from anything beyond, as the painting exists by virtue of its frame.* Just as the picture is not to be confounded with the scene it represents and is not a window in a wall. The stage and the decor where the action unfolds constitute an aesthetic microcosm inserted perforce into the universe but essentially distinct from the Nature which surrounds it.

It is not the same with cinema, the basic principle of which is a denial of any frontiers to action.

The idea of a *locus dramaticus* is not only alien to, it is essentially a contradiction of the concept of the screen. The screen is not a frame like that of a picture but a mask which allows only a part of the action to be seen. When a character moves off screen, we accept the fact that he is out of sight, but he continues to exist in his own capacity at some other place in the decor which is hidden from us. There are no wings to the screen. There could not be without destroying its specific illusion, which is to make of a revolver or of a face the very center of the universe. In contrast to the stage the space of the screen is centrifugal. It is because that infinity which the theater demands cannot be spatial that its area can be none

---

* The ideal historical example of this theory of theater architecture and its relations to the stage and the decor is provided by the Palladium with the extraordinary Olympic Theater of Vicenza, making of the ancient amphitheater open to the sky a purely architectural *trompe-l'oeil*. There is not a single element, including the entrance to the auditorium, which is not an affirmation of its essentially architectural nature. Built in 1590, inside an old barracks donated by the town, outwardly the Olympic Theater appears to be just red-brick walls, that is, a purely utilitarian piece of architecture which one might describe as amorphous in the sense in which chemists distinguish between the amorphous state and the crystal state of the same body. The visitor going in by what appears to be a hole in the wall cannot believe his eyes when he finds himself all of a sudden in the extraordinary hollowed-out grotto which constitutes the semicircle of the theater. Like those blocks of quartz or amethyst which outwardly look like common stones whereas inside they are a composite of pure crystal, secretly oriented inward, the theater of Vicenza is conceived according to the laws of an aesthetic and artificial space polarized exclusively towards the center.

other than the human soul. Enclosed in this space the actor is at the focus of a two-fold concave mirror. From the auditorium and from the decor there converge on him the dim lights of conscious human beings and of the footlights themselves. But the fire with which he burns is at once that of his inner passion and of that focal point at which he stands. He lights up in each member of his audience an accomplice flame. Like the ocean in a sea shell the dramatic infinities of the human heart moan and beat between the enclosing walls of the theatrical sphere. This is why this dramaturgy is in its essence human. Man is at once its cause and its subject.

On the screen man is no longer the focus of the drama, but will become eventually the center of the universe. The impact of his action may there set in motion an infinitude of waves. The decor that surrounds him is part of the solidity of the world. For this reason the actor as such can be absent from it, because man in the world enjoys no a priori privilege over animals and things. However there is no reason why he should not be the mainspring of the drama, as in Dreyer's *Jeanne d'Arc,* and in this respect the cinema may very well impose itself upon the theater. As actions *Phèdre* or *King Lear* are no less cinematogaphic than theatrical, and the visible death of a rabbit in *La Règle du jeu* affects us just as deeply as that of Agnès' little cat about which we are merely told.

But if Racine, Shakespeare, or Molière cannot be brought to the cinema by just placing them before the camera and the microphone, it is because the handling of the action and the style of the dialogue were conceived as echoing through the architecture of the auditorium. What is specifically theatrical about these tragedies is not their action so much as the human, that is to say the verbal, priority given to their dramatic structure. The problem of filmed theater at least where the classics are concerned does not consist so much in transposing an action from the stage to the screen as in transposing a text written for one dramaturgical system into another while at the same time retaining its effectiveness. It is not therefore essentially the action of a play which resists film adaptation, but above and beyond the phases of the intrigue (which it would be easy enough to adapt to the realism of the screen) it is the verbal form which aesthetic contingencies or cultural prejudices oblige us to respect. It is this which refuses to let itself be captured in the window of the screen. "The theater," says Baudelaire, "is a crystal chandelier." If one were called upon to offer in comparison a symbol other than this artificial crystal-like object, brilliant, intricate, and circular, which refracts the light which plays around its center and holds us prisoners of its aureole, we might say of the cinema that it is the little flashlight of the usher, moving like an uncertain comet across the night of our waking dream, the diffuse space without shape or frontiers that surrounds the screen.

The story of the failures and recent successes of theater on film will be found to be that of the ability of directors to retain the dramatic force of the play in a medium that reflects it or, at least, the ability to give this dramatic force enough resonance to permit a film audience to perceive it. In other words, it is a matter of an aesthetic that is not concerned with the actor but with decor and editing. Henceforth it is clear that filmed theater is basically destined to fail whenever it tends in any manner to become simply the photographing of scenic representation even and perhaps most of all when the camera is used to try and make us forget the footlights and the backstage area. The dramatic force of the text, instead of being gathered up in the actor, dissolves without echo into the cinematic ether. This is why a filmed play can show due respect to the text, be well acted in likely settings, and yet be completely worthless. This is what happened, to take a convenient example, to *Le Voyageur sans baggages*. The play lies there before us apparently true to itself yet drained of every ounce of energy, like a battery dead from an unknown short. But over and beyond the aesthetic of the decor we see clearly both on the screen and on the stage that in the last analysis the problem before us is that of realism. This is the problem we always end up with when we are dealing with cinema.

The Screen and the Realism of Space

The realism of the cinema follows directly from its photographic nature. Not only does some marvel or some fantastic thing on the screen not undermine the reality of the image, on the contrary it is its most valid justification. Illusion in the cinema is not based as it is in the theater on convention tacitly accepted by the general public; rather, contrariwise, it is based on the inalienable realism of that which is shown. All trick work must be perfect in all material respects on the screen. The "invisible man" must wear pyjamas and smoke a cigarette.

Must we conclude from this that the cinema is dedicated entirely to the representation if not of natural reality at least of a plausible reality of which the spectator admits the identity with nature as he knows it? The comparative failure of German expressionism would seem to confirm this hypothesis, since it is evident that *Caligari* attempted to depart from realistic decor under the influence of the theater and painting. But this would be to offer an oversimplified explanation for a problem that calls for more subtle answers. We are prepared to admit that the screen opens upon an artificial world provided there exists a common denominator between the cinematographic image and the world we live in. Our experience of space is the structural basis for our concept of the universe. We may say in fact, adapting Henri Gouhier's formula, "the stage welcomes every illusion except the illusion of presence," that "the cinematographic image can be emptied of all reality save one—the reality of space."

It is perhaps an overstatement to say "all reality" because it is difficult to imagine a reconstruction of space devoid of all reference to nature. The world of the screen and our world cannot be juxtaposed. The screen of necessity substitutes for it since the very concept of universe is spatially exclusive. For a time, a film is the Universe, the world, or if you like, Nature. We will see how the films that have attempted to substitute a fabricated nature and an artificial world for the world of experience have not all equally succeeded. Admitting the failure of *Caligari* and *Die Nibelungen* we then ask ourselves how we explain the undoubted success of *Nosferatu* and *La Passion de Jeanne d'Arc,* the criterion of success being that these films have never aged. Yet it would seem at first sight that the methods of direction belong to the same aesthetic family, and that viewing the varieties of temperament and period, one could group these four films together as expressionist as distinct from realist. However, if we examine them more closely we see that there are certain basic differences between them. It is clear in the case of R. Weine and Murnau. *Nosferatu* plays, for the greater part of the time, against natural settings whereas the fantastic qualities of *Caligari* are derived from deformities of lighting and decor. The case of Dreyer's *Jeanne d'Arc* is a little more subtle since at first sight nature plays a nonexistent role. To put it more directly, the decor by Jean Hugo is no whit less artificial and theatrical than the settings of *Caligari;* the systematic use of close-ups and unusual angles is well calculated to destroy any sense of space. Regular cinéclub goers know that the film is unfailingly introduced with the famous story of how the hair of Falconetti was actually cut in the interests of the film and likewise, the actors, we are told, wore no make-up. These references to history ordinarily have no more than gossip value. In this case, they seem to me to hold the aesthetic secret of the film; the very thing to which it owes its continued survival. It is precisely because of them that the work of Dreyer ceases to have anything in common with the theater, and indeed one might say, with man. The greater recourse Dreyer has exclusively to the human "expression," the more he has to reconvert it again into Nature. Let there be no mistake, that prodigious fresco of heads is the very opposite of an actor's film. It is a documentary of faces. It is not important how well the actors play, whereas the pockmarks on Bishop Cauchon's face and the red patches of Jean d'Yd are an integral part of the action. In this drama-through-the-microscope the whole of nature palpitates beneath every pore. The movement of a wrinkle, the pursing of a lip are seismic shocks and the flow of tides, the flux and reflux of this human epidermis. But for me Dreyer's brilliant sense of cinema is evidenced in the exterior scene which every other director would assuredly have shot in the studio. The decor as built evoked a Middle Ages of the theater and of miniatures. In one sense, nothing is less realistic than this tribunal in the cemetery or this drawbridge, but the whole is lit by the light of the sun and the gravedigger throws a spadeful of real earth into the hole.*

It is these "secondary" details, apparently aesthetically at odds with the rest of the work, which give it its truly cinematic quality.

If the paradox of the cinema is rooted in the dialectic of concrete and abstract, if cinema is committed to communicate only by way of what is real, it becomes all the more important to discern those elements in filming which confirm our sense of natural reality and those which destroy that feeling. On the other hand, it certainly argues a lack of perception to derive one's sense of reality from these accumulations of factual detail. It is possible to argue that *Les Dames du Bois de Boulogne* is an eminently realistic film, though everything about it is stylized. Everything, except for the rarely noticeable sound of a windshield-wiper, the murmur of a waterfall, or the rushing sound of soil escaping from a broken vase. These are the noises, chosen precisely for their "indifference" to the action, that guarantee its reality.

The cinema being of its essence a dramaturgy of Nature, there can be no cinema without the setting up of an open space in place of the universe rather than as part of it. The screen cannot give us

---

* This is why I consider the graveyard scene in *Hamlet* and the death of Ophelia bad mistakes on Olivier's part. He had here a chance to introduce sun and soil by way of counterpoint to the setting of Elsinore. Does the actual shot of the sea during the soliloquy of Hamlet show that he had sensed the need for this? The idea, excellent in itself, is not well handled technically.

the illusion of this feeling of space without calling on certain natural guarantees. But it is less a question of set construction or of architecture or of immensity than of isolating the aesthetic catalyst, which it is sufficient to introduce in an infinitesimal dose, to have it immediately take on the reality of nature.

The concrete forest of *Die Nibelungen* may well pretend to be an infinite expanse. We do not believe it to be so, whereas the trembling of just one branch in the wind, and the sunlight, would be enough to conjure up all the forests of the world.

If this analysis be well founded, then we see that the basic aesthetic problem of filmed theater is indeed that of the decor. The trump card that the director must hold is the reconversion into a window onto the world of a space oriented toward an interior dimension only, namely the closed and conventional area of the theatrical play.

It is not in Laurence Olivier's *Hamlet* that the text seems to be rendered superfluous or its strength diminished by directorial interpretations, still less in Welles' *Macbeth,* but paradoxically in the stage productions of Gaston Baty, to the precise extent that they go out of their way to create a cinematographic space on the stage; to deny that the settings have a reverse side, thus reducing the sonority of the text simply to the vibration of the voice of the actor who is left without his "resonance box" like a violin that is nothing else but strings. One would never deny that the essential thing in the theater is the text. The latter conceived for the anthropocentric expression proper to the stage and having as its function to bring nature to it cannot, without losing its raison d'être, be used in a space transparent as glass. The problem then that faces the filmmaker is to give his decor a dramatic opaqueness while at the same time reflecting its natural realism. Once this paradox of space has been dealt with, the director, so far from hesitating to bring theatrical conventions and faithfulness to the text to the screen will find himself now, on the contrary, completely free to rely on them. From that point on it is no longer a matter of running away from

111

those things which "make theater" but in the long run to acknowledge their existence by rejecting the resources of the cinema, as
Cocteau did in *Les Parents terribles* and Welles in *Macbeth,* or by
putting them in quotation marks as Laurence Olivier did in *Henry
V.* The evidence of a return to filmed theater that we have had
during the last ten years belongs essentially to the history of decor
and editing. It is a conquest of realism—not, certainly, the realism
of subject matter or realism of expression but that realism of space
without which moving pictures do not constitute cinema.

An Analogy from Play-Acting

This progress in filmed theater has only been possible insofar as the
opposition between them did not rest on the ontological category of
presence but on a psychology of "play." In passing from one to the
other, one goes from the absolute to the relative, from antinomy to
simple contradiction. While the cinema cannot offer the spectator
the community feeling of theater, a certain knowledge of direction
will allow him finally, and this is a decisive factor, to preserve the
meaning and force of the text. The grafting of the theatrical text
onto the decor of cinema is an operation which today we know can
be successful. There remains that awareness of the active opposition existing between the spectator and the actor which constitutes
the "play" of theater and is symbolized by scenic architecture. But
there is a way of reducing even this to the psychology of the cinematic.

The reasoning of Rosenkrantz concerning opposition and identification requires in effect an important correction. It carries with it,
still, a measure of equivocation. Rosenkrantz seems to equate identification with passivity and escape—an accepted fact in his time because of the condition of the cinema but less and less so in its present stage of evolution. Actually the cinema of myth and dream is

now only one variety of production and one that is less and less frequent. One must not confuse an accidental and historical social condition with an unalterable psychological one—two activities, that is to say, of the spectator's consciousness that converge but are not part of one another. I do not identify equally with Tarzan and Bresson's curé. The only denominator common to my attitude to these two heroes is that I believe that they really exist, that I cannot refuse, except by staying away from the film, to share their adventures and to live them through with them, inside their universe, a universe that is not metaphorical and figurative but spatially real. This interior sharing does not exclude, in the second example, a consciousness of myself as distinct from the person from whom I chose to be alienated in the first example. These factors originating in the affective order are not the only ones that argue against passive identification; films like *L'Espoir* or *Citizen Kane* require in the spectator an intellectual alertness incompatible with passivity. The most that one can suggest is that the psychology of the cinematographic image offers a natural incline leading towards a sociology of the hero characterized by a passive identification. But in the arts as in morals, inclines are also made to be climbed. While the contemporary man of the theater often tries to lessen the sense of theatricality in a performance by a kind of realism in the production—just as those who love to go to the Grand Guignol play at being frightened but hold on at the very height of the horror to a delicious awareness of being fooled—the film director discovers on his side means of exciting the awareness of the spectator and of provoking him to reflection. This is something which would set up a conflict at the very heart of the identification. This private zone of consciousness, this self-awareness at the height of illusion, creates a kind of private footlights. In filmed theater it is no longer the microcosm of the play which is set over against nature but the spectator who is conscious of himself. On the screen *Hamlet* and *Les Parents terribles* cannot nor should they escape from the laws of cinematic perception; Elsinore and "La Roulotte" really exist but

113

I pass through them unseen, rejoicing in that equivocal freedom which certain dreams allow us. I am walking but moving backwards.

Certainly the possibility of a state of intellectual self-awareness at the moment of psychological identification should never be confused with that act of the will which constitutes theater, and that is why it is foolish to identify stage and screen as Pagnol does. No matter how conscious of myself, how intelligent a film can make me, it is not to my will that it appeals—only at most to my good will. A film calls for a certain effort on my part so that I may understand and enjoy it, but it does not depend on me for its existence. Nevertheless it would certainly seem, from experience, that the margin of awareness allowed by the cinema is enough to establish an acceptable equivalent to the pleasure given by theater, at least enough to preserve what is essential to the artistic values of the play. The film, while it cannot pretend to be a complete substitute for the stage performance, is at least capable of assuring the theater a valid artistic existence and can offer us a comparable pleasure. There can never be question of anything more than a complex mechanical aesthetic where the original theatrical effectiveness is almost never directly applied, rather it is preserved, reconstituted, and transmitted thanks to a system of circuits, as in *Henry V,* of amplification as for example in *Macbeth,* of induction or interference. The true filmed theater is not the phonograph, it is its Martenot wave.

Morality

Thus the practice (certain) like the theory (possible) of successful filmed theater reveals the reasons for former failures. Straightforward animated photography of theater is a childish error recognized as such these thirty years and on which there is no point in insisting further. The heresy of film adaptation has taken longer to smoke out. It will continue to have its dupes but we now know where it leads—to aesthetic limbos that belong neither to film nor to theater, to that "filmed theater" justly condemned as the sin against the spirit of cinema. The true solution, revealed at last, consists in realizing that it is not a matter of transferring to the screen the dramatic element—an element interchangeable between one art and another—of a theatrical work, but inversely the theatrical quality of the drama. The subject of the adaptation is not that of the play, it is the play precisely in its scenic essence. This truth, apparent at last, will allow us to reach a conclusion concerning three propositions seemingly paradoxical at first, but which on reflection are seen to be quite evident.

(1) Theater an Aid to Cinema

The first proposition is that so far from being a corruption of cinema, filmed theater serves on the contrary to enrich and elevate it. Let us first look at the matter of theater. It is alas only too certain that the level of film production is intellectually much below, if not that of current dramatic production—think of Jean de Létraz and Henry Bernstein—at least of the living heritage of theater, even if only because of its great age. True, our century is no less that of Charlie Chaplin than was the seventeenth century that of Racine and Molière, but after all the cinema has only half a century of literature behind it while the theater has twenty-five. What would the French theater be like today if, as is the case with the cinema, it had nothing to offer but the production of the past decade? Since the cinema is undeniably passing through a crisis of subject matter it is not risking anything by employing screen writers like Shakespeare or even Feydeau. Let us not labor the subject. The case is only too clear. However, the inferiority is less evident in the realm of form. If the cinema is a major art with its own laws and language, what can it gain by submitting to the laws and language of another art? A great deal! And precisely to the extent to which, laying aside all its vain and puerile tricks, it is seriously concerned to subordinate itself and render a service. To justify this point of view completely, one should really discuss it within the framework of the aesthetic history of influence in art in general. This would almost certainly reveal, we feel, that at some stage in their evolution there has been a definite commerce between the technique of the various arts. Our prejudice about "pure art" is a critical development of relatively recent origin. But the authority of these precedents is not indispensable to our argument. The art of direction, the mechanics of which in relation to certain major films, as we have had to explain earlier, more even than our theoretical hypotheses, supposes on the part of the director a grasp of the language of cinematography equalled only by his knowledge of what theater is. If the *film d'art* failed where Olivier and Cocteau have succeeded, it is first of all because they have at their disposal a much more developed means of expression, but they also know how to use it more effectively than their contemporaries. To say of *Les Parents terribles* that it is perhaps an excellent film but that it is not cinema because it follows the play step by step is critical nonsense. On the contrary, it is precisely for this reason that it is cinema. It is *Topaze* by Marcel Pagnol—in its most recent style—which is not cinema, precisely because it is no longer theater. There is more cinema, and great cinema at that, in *Henry V* alone than in 90% of original scripts. Pure poetry is certainly not that which has nothing to say, as Cocteau has so well demonstrated: all the examples of pure poetry given by the Abbé Brémond illustrate the exact opposite. *La Fille de Minos et Pasiphae* is as informative as a birth certificate. There is likewise a way, unfortunately not yet practiced, of reciting this poem on the screen which would be pure cinema because it would respect, in the most intelligent way, its true theatrical value.

The more the cinema intends to be faithful to the text and to its theatrical requirements, the more of necessity must it delve deeper into its own language. The best translation is that which demonstrates a close intimacy with the genius of both languages and, likewise, a mastery of both.

(2) *The Cinema Will Save the Theater*

That is why the cinema will give back to the theater unstintingly what it took from her, if it has not already done so. For if the success of filmed theater supposes that dialectical progress had been made with the cinematic form, it implies both reciprocally and a fortiori a reevaluation of the essentially theatrical. The idea exploited by Marcel Pagnol according to which the cinema will replace the theater by "canning it" is completely false. The screen cannot replace the stage as the piano has supplanted the clavichord. And to begin with, replace the theater for whom? Not for the film-going public that long ago deserted the theater. The divorce between public and theater does not date, so far as I know, from that historic evening at the Grand Café in 1895. Are we talking then about the privileged minority of culture and wealth which actually makes up the theater audiences? But we see that Jean de Létraz is not bankrupt and that the visitor to Paris from the provinces does not confuse the breasts of Françoise Arnoul that he has seen on the screen with those of Nathalie Nattier at the Palais-Royal, although the latter may be covered by a brassière; but they are there, if I may say so, "in the flesh." Ah! The irreplaceable presence of the actor! As for the "serious" theaters, say the Marigny or the Français, it is clearly a question of a public that, for the most part, does not go to the cinema and, for the others, of people who go to both without confusing the pleasure to be derived from each. The fact is, if any ground has been taken over it is not the territory of the theatrical spectacle as it exists, it is much more the taking over of the place abandoned long ago by the now-defunct forms of popular theater. So far from being a serious rival to the stage, the cinema is in process of giving back, to a public that had lost it, a taste and feeling for theater.*

It is possible that canned theater had something to do at the time with the disappearance of touring companies from the road. When Marcel Pagnol makes a film of *Topaze,* there is no doubt about his intentions, namely to make his play available to the provinces with a "Paris cast" at the price of a cinema seat. It is often the same with the boulevard plays. Their successful run finished, the film is distributed to those who were unable to see the play. In those areas where the Baret touring companies performed with a second-rate cast, the film offers at a very reasonable price not only the original cast, but even more magnificent sets. But this illusion was really successful for only a few years and we now see provincial tours on the road again, the better for their experience. The public they have recaptured, made blasé by the cinema and its glamorous casting and its luxurious sets, has, "come to," as they say, and is looking for something that is, more or less, theater.

But the popularizing of Paris successes is still not the ultimate end of the theatrical revival nor is it the chief merit of the "competition" between screen and stage. One might even say that this improvement in the situation of the touring companies is due to badly filmed theater. It is the defects of these films that have finally turned the stomachs of a section of the public and sent them back into the theaters.

---

* The case of the Théâtre Nationale Populaire offers another unexpected and paradoxical example of support for the theater by the cinema. I presume that Jean Vilar would not dispute the undoubted help his enterprise gets from the film fame of Gérard Philipe. Actually in doing this the cinema is only paying back to the theater a part of the capital it borrowed some forty years ago in the heroic period when the infant film industry, an object of contempt, had recourse to stage celebrities who could provide the artistic discipline and prestige it needed before it could be taken seriously. Certainly the situation was soon enough reversed. The Sarah Bernhardt of the years between the wars went by the name of Greta Garbo and it is now the theater that is willing to advertise the name of a film star on its marquees.

It was the same situation with regard to photography and paint-ing. Photography freed painting from what was aesthetically least essential to it: likeness and anecdote. The high standard and the lower cost of photography and the ease with which pictures are taken, has at last contributed to the due evaluation of painting and to establishing it unalterably in its proper place. But this is not the end of the benefits derived from their coexistence. The photogra-phers have not just served as the helots of the painters. At the same time, as it became more conscious of itself, painting absorbed some-thing of photography. It is Degas and Toulouse-Lautrec, Renoir and Manet, who have understood from the inside, and in essence, the nature of the photographic phenomenon and, prophetically, even the cinematographic phenomenon. Faced with photography, they opposed it in the only valid way, by a dialectical enriching of pictorial technique. They understood the laws of the new image better than the photographers and well before the movie-makers, and it is they who first applied them.

Nevertheless this is not all and photography is in process of rendering services to the plastic arts that are even more decisive still. Their fields henceforth clearly known and delimited, the auto-matic image multiplies and renews our knowledge of the pictorial image. Malraux has said what needed to be said on this. If painting has been able to become the most individual of arts, the most onerous, the most independent of all compromise while at the same time the most accessible, it is thanks to color photography.

The same process applies to the theater; bad "canned theater" has helped true theater to become aware of its own laws. The cinema has likewise contributed to a new concept of theatrical production. These are results henceforth firmly established. But there is a third result which good filmed theater permits us to look for, namely the remarkable increase in breadth of understanding of theater among the general public. What then is a film like *Henry V?* First of all, it is Shakespeare for everybody. Furthermore, and su-premely, it is a blazing light thrown onto the dramatic poetry of

Shakespeare—the most effective and brilliant of theater lessons. Shakespeare emerges from the process twice himself. Not only does the adaptation of the play multiply his potential audience in the same way that the adaptation of novels makes the fortune of publishers, but also, the public is far better prepared than before to enjoy the stage play. Laurence Olivier's *Hamlet* must obviously increase the audience for Jean-Louis Barrault's *Hamlet* and sharpen the critical sense. Just as there is a difference that can never be bridged between the finest modern reproduction of a painting and the pleasure of owning the original, seeing Hamlet on the screen cannot take the place of a performance of the play by, say, a group of English students. But you need a genuine education in theater to appreciate the real-life performance by amateurs, that is to be able truly to share in what they are doing. So the more successful the filmed theater, the deeper it probes into the essence of theater, the better to serve it, the more clearly it will reveal the unbridgeable gulf between stage and screen. It is, on the contrary, the canned theater on the one hand and mediocre popular theater on the other that give rise to the confusion. *Les Parents terribles* never misleads its audience. There is not a sequence in it that is not more effective than its stage counterpart, while there is not one which does not allude by implication to that indefinable pleasure that I would have had from the real thing. There is no better propaganda for the real theater than well-filmed theater. These truths are henceforth indisputable and it would have been ridiculous of me to have spent so much time on them if the myth about filmed theater did not still survive too frequently in the form of prejudice, of misunderstanding, and of minds already made up.

(3) *From Filmed Theater to Cinematographic Theater*

My last argument, I realize, will be the boldest. So far we have considered the theater as an aesthetic absolute to which the cinema can come close in a more or less satisfactory fashion, but only in all circumstances and under the best possible conditions, as its humble servant. However, the earlier part of our study allowed us to see in slapstick the rebirth of dramatic forms that had practically disappeared, such as farce and the *Commedia dell'Arte*. Certain dramatic situations, certain techniques that had degenerated in the course of time, found again, in the cinema, first the sociological nourishment they needed to survive and, still better, the conditions favorable to an expansive use of their aesthetic, which the theater had kept congenitally atrophied. In making a protagonist out of space, the screen does not betray the spirit of farce, it simply gives to the metaphysical meaning of Scarpin's stick its true dimensions, namely those of the whole universe. Slapstick is first and foremost, or at least is also, the dramatic expression of the tyranny of things, out of which Keaton even more than Chaplin knew how to create a tragedy of the Object. But it is true that the forms of comedy create something of a special problem in the history of filmed theater, probably because laughter allows the audience to become aware of itself and to use this to experience a measure of the opposition that theater creates between actor and audience. In any case, and that is why we have not gone farther into the study of it, the grafting together of cinema and comedy-theater happened spontaneously and has been so perfect that its fruit has always been accepted as the product of pure cinema.

Now that the screen can welcome other kinds of theater besides comedy without betraying them, there is no reason to suppose that it cannot likewise give the theater new life, employing certain of the stage's own techniques. Film cannot be, indeed must not be, as we have seen, simply a paradoxical modality of theater production, but stage structures have their importance and it is not a matter of indifference whether *Julius Caesar* is played in the arena at Nîmes or in a studio; but certain dramatic works, and by no means the least of them, have suffered in a very material way these thirty to fifty years from a discord between contemporary taste and the style of the staging that they call for. I am thinking particularly of tragedy. There, the handicap we suffer from is due especially to the disappearance of the race of traditional tragedians of the old school—the Mounet-Sullys and the Sarah Bernhardts, that is, who disappeared at the beginning of the century like prehistoric creatures of the secondary period. By a stroke of irony, it is the cinema that has preserved their bones, fossilized in the *films d'art*. It has become a commonplace to attribute their disappearance to the cinema and for two converging reasons: one aesthetic, the other sociological. The screen has certainly modified our feeling about verisimilitude in interpretation. It is enough to see one of the little films of Bernhardt or Bargy to understand that this type of actor was still trussed up to all intents and purposes in cothurnus and mask. But the mask is simply an object of laughter while a close-up can drown us in a tear, and the megaphone is ridiculous when the microphone can produce at will a roar from the feeblest vocal chords. Thus we are accustomed to the inner naturalness which only allows the stage actor a slender margin of stylization beyond verisimilitude. The sociological factor is probably even more decisive. The success and effectiveness of a Mounet-Sully was undoubtedly due to his talent but helped on by the consenting complicity of the public. It was the phenomenon of the *monstre sacré* which is today diverted almost exclusively to the cinema. To say that the classes at the Conservatory do not produce any more tragedians doesn't by any means imply that no more Sarah Bernhardts are being born, only that their gifts and the times do not consort well. Thus, Voltaire wore out his lungs plagiarizing the tragedy of the seventeenth century because he thought that it was only Racine who had died when actually it was tragedy itself. Today we see not the slightest difference between Mounet-Sully and a ham from the provinces because we could not recognize a tragedian of the old school when we saw one. Only the "monster" survives in the *film d'art* for a young man today. The sacred quality has departed.

In the circumstances it is not surprising that Racine's tragedy is in a period of eclipse. Thanks to its conservative attitude, the

Comédie Française is in the fortunate position of being able to guarantee him a reasonable life, but no longer a triumphal one.* Furthermore, this is only because of an interesting filtering-through of traditional values, their delicate adaptation to modern tastes, and not by a radical renewal straight out of the period. As for ancient tragedy, it is paradoxically to the Sorbonne and to the archeological enthusiasm of students that it owes the fact that it moves us once more. But it is important to see in these experiments by amateurs an extremely radical reaction against the actor's theater.

Thus, is it not natural to think that if the cinema has completely turned to its own advantage the aesthetic and the sociology of the sacred monster, that it might return them if the theater came looking for them? It is reasonable enough to dream what an Athalie could have been with Yvonne de Bray and Jean Cocteau directing!

But doubtless it would not be just the style of the interpretation of tragedy that would find its raison d'être once more on the screen. One could well imagine a corresponding revolution on the stage which, without ceasing to be faithful to the spirit of the theater, would offer it new forms in keeping with modern taste and especially at the level of a great mass audience. Film theater is waiting for a Jean Cocteau to make it a cinematographic theater.

Thus not only is theater on film from now on aesthetically founded in truth and fact, not only do we know that henceforth there are no plays that cannot be brought to the screen, whatever their style, provided one can visualize a reconversion of stage space in accordance with the data. But it may also be that the only possible modern theatrical production of certain classics would be on the screen. It is no chance matter that some of the best filmmakers are also the best stage directors. Welles and Olivier did not

---

* Triumph is precisely what *Henry V* is, thanks to color film. If one were searching through *Phèdre* for an example of cinematic potentiality, the recital of Theramine, a verbal reminiscence of the *tragicomédie à machines,* considered as a dramatically literary piece, dramatically out of place, would find, visually, a new raison d'être on the screen.

come to the cinema out of cynicism, snobbery, or ambition, not even, like Pagnol, to popularize theatrical works. Cinema is for them only a complementary form of theater, the chance to produce theater precisely as they feel and see it.

LE JOURNAL D'UN CURÉ DE CAMPAGNE
AND THE STYLISTICS OF ROBERT BRESSON

IF *The Diary of a Country Priest* impresses us as a masterpiece, and this with an almost physical impact, if it moves the critic and the uncritical alike, it is primarily because of its power to stir the emotions, rather than the intelligence, at their highest level of sensitivity. The temporary eclipse of *Les Dames du Bois de Boulogne* was for precisely the opposite reason. This film could not stir us unless we had, if not exactly analyzed, at least tested its intellectual structure and, so to speak, understood the rules of the game.

While the instantaneous success of *Le Journal* is undeniable, the aesthetic principles on which it is based are nevertheless the most paradoxical, maybe even the most complex, ever manifest in a sound film. Hence the refrain of those critics, ill-equipped to understand it. "Paradoxical," they say, "incredible—an unprecedented success that can never be repeated." Thus they renounce any attempt at explanation and take refuge in the perfect alibi of a stroke of genius. On the other hand, among those whose aesthetic preferences are of a kind with Bresson's and whom one would have unhesitatingly thought to be his allies, there is a deep sense of disappointment in proportion as they expected greater acts of daring from him.

First embarrassed, then irritated by the realization of what the director did not do, yet too long in accord with him to be able to change their views on the spot; too caught up in his style to recapture their intellectual virginity which would have left the way open to emotion, they have neither understood nor liked the film.

Thus we find the critical field divided into two extreme groups. At one end those least equipped to understand *Le Journal* and who, by the same token, have loved it all the more without knowing why; at the other end those "happy few" who, expecting something different, have not liked it and have failed to understand it. It is the strangers to the cinema, the men of letters, amazed that they could so love a film and be capable of freeing their minds of prejudice, who have understood what Bresson had in mind more clearly than anyone else.

Admittedly Bresson has done his best to cover his tracks. His avowal of fidelity to the original from the first moment that he embarked on the adaptation, his declared intention of following the book word-for-word conditioned us to look for just that and the film only serves to prove it. Unlike Aurenche and Bost, who were preoccupied with the optics of the screen and the balance of their drama in its new form, Bresson, instead of building up the minor characters like the parents in *Le Diable au corps,* eliminated them. He prunes even the very essentials, giving an impression as he does so of a fidelity unable to sacrifice one single word without a pucker of concern and a thousand preliminary twinges of remorse. Again this pruning is always in the interest of simplification, never of addition. It is no exaggeration to say that if Bernanos had written the screenplay he would have taken greater liberties with his novel. He had, indeed, explicitly recognized the right of the adaptor to make use of his book according to the requirements of the cinema, the right that is "to dream his story over."

However, if we praise Bresson for his fidelity, it is for the most insidious kind of fidelity, a most pervasive form of creative license. Of course, one clearly cannot adapt without transposing. In that respect, Bernanos was on the side of aesthetic common sense. Literal translations are not the faithful ones. The changes that Aurenche and Bost made to *Le Diable au corps* are almost all entirely justified in principle. A character on the screen and the same character as evoked by the novelist are not identical.

Valéry condemned the novel for being obliged to record that "the Marquise had tea at five o'clock." On his side, the novelist might in turn pity the film-maker for having to show the marquise actually at the table. It is for this reason that the relatives of the heroes in Radiguet, peripheral in the novel, appear important on the screen. The adaptor, however, must be as concerned with the text as with the characters and with the threat of their physical presence to the balance of the story. Having transformed the narrative into visuals, the film-maker must put the rest into dialogue, including the existing dialogue of the novel although we expect some modification of the latter—since spoken as written, its effectiveness and even its meaning will normally evaporate.

It is here that we see the paradoxical effect of the textual fidelity of *Le Journal*.

While the characters in the book are presented to the reader in high relief and while their inevitably brief evocation by the pen of the curé of Ambricourt never gives us a feeling of frustration or of any limits being put both to their existence and to our knowledge of their existence, Bresson, in the process of showing them to us, is forever hurrying them out of sight. In place of the powerfully concrete evocations of the novelist, the film offers us an increasingly impoverished image which escapes us because it is hidden from us and is never really developed.

The novel of Bernanos is rich in picturesque evocations, solid, concrete, strikingly visual. For example: "The Count went out—his excuse the rain. With every step the water oozed from his long boots. The three or four rabbits he had shot were lumped together in the bottom of his game-bag in a horrible-looking little pile of bloodstained mud and grey hair. He had hung the string bag on the

127

wall and as he talked to me I saw fixed on me, through the intertwining cords, a still limpid and gentle eye."

Do you feel you have seen all this somewhere before? Don't bother to look where. It was probably in a Renoir film. Now compare this scene with the other in which the count brings the two rabbits to the presbytery—admittedly this comes later in the book but the two could have profitably been combined, thus giving them a style in common—and if you still have any doubts, Bresson's own admission will remove them. Forced to throw out a third of his final cut for the exhibitor's copy he ended, as we know, by declaring with a delicate touch of cynicism that he was delighted to have had to do so. Actually, the only "visual" he really cared about was the blank screen at the finale, which we will discuss later.

If he had really been faithful to the book, Bresson would have made quite a different film. Determined though he was to add nothing to the original—already a subtle form of betrayal by omission—he might at least have chosen to sacrifice the more literary parts for the many passages of ready-made film material that cried out for visualization. Yet he systematically took the opposite course. When you compare the two, it is the film that is literary while the novel teems with visual material.

The way he handles the text is even more revealing. He refuses to put into dialogue (I hardly dare to say "film dialogue") those passages from the novel where the curé enters in his diary the report of such-and-such a conversation. Here is a first discrepancy, since Bernanos at no point guarantees that the curé is giving a word for word report of what he heard. The odds are that he is not. In any event, supposing he *is,* and that Bresson has it in mind to preserve, along with the objective image, the subjective character of something remembered, it is still true that the mental and emotional impact of a line that is merely read is very different from that of a spoken line.

Now, not only does he not adapt the dialogue, however circumspectly, to the demands of a performance, he goes out of his way, on the contrary, whenever the text of the novel has the rhythm and balance of true dialogue, to prevent the actor from bringing out these qualities. Thus a good deal of excellent dramatic dialogue is thrown away because of the flat monotone in which the director insists that it be delivered.

Many complimentary things have been said about *Les Dames du Bois de Boulogne,* very little about the adaptation. The critics have, to all intents and purposes, treated the film as if it was made from an original screenplay. The outstanding quality of the dialogue has been attributed to Cocteau, whose reputation has little need of such praise. This is because they have not reread *Jacques le fataliste,* in which they would have found if not the entire script, at least the evidence of a subtle game of hide and go seek, word for word, with the text of Diderot. While it did not make one feel one ought to go back to verify the fact at close quarters, the modern version left one with the impression that Bresson had taken liberties with the story and retained simply the situation and, if you like, a certain eighteenth-century flavor. Since, in addition, he had killed off two or three writers under him, so to speak, it was reasonable to suppose that he was that many steps away from the original. However I recommend fans of the *Dames du Bois de Boulogne* and aspiring scenarists alike to take a second look at the film with these considerations in mind. Without intending in any way to detract from the decisive part played by the style of the direction in the success of the film, it is important to examine very closely the foundations of this success, namely a marvellously subtle interplay—a sort of counterpoint between faithfulness and unfaithfulness to the original.

It has been suggested in criticism of *Les Dames du Bois de Boulogne,* with equal proportions of good sense and misunderstanding, that the psychological make-up of the characters is out of key with the society in which they are shown as living. True, it is the mores of the time that, in the novel of Diderot, justify the choice of the revenge and give it its effectiveness. It is true again that this same revenge seems to the modern spectator to be something out of the blue, something beyond his experience. It is equally useless on the other hand for those who defend the film to look for any sort of social justification for the characters. Prostitution and pandering as shown in the novel are facts with a very clear and solid contemporary social context. In the film of *Les Dames* they are all the more mystifying since they have no basic justification. The revenge of an injured mistress who forces her unfaithful lover to marry a luscious cabaret dancer seems to us to be a ridiculous gesture. Nor can the fact that the characters appear to be abstractions be explained by deliberate cuts made by the director during the filming. They are that way in the script. The reason Bresson does not tell us more about his characters is not because he has no desire to, but because he would be hard put to do so. Racine does not describe the color of the wall paper in the rooms to which his characters retire. To this one may answer, of course, that classical tragedy has no need of the alibis of realism and that this is one of the basic differences between the theater and the cinema. That is true enough. It is also precisely why Bresson does not derive his cinematographic abstraction simply from the bare episodes but from the counterpoint that the reality of the situation sets up with itself. In *Les Dames du Bois de Boulogne,* Bresson has taken the risk of transferring one realistic story into the context of another. The result is that these two examples of realism cancel one another out, the passions displayed emerge out of the characters as if from a chrysalis, the action from the twists and turns of the plot, and the tragedy from the trappings of the drama. The sound of a windshield-wiper against a page of Diderot is all it took to turn it into Racinian dialogue. Obviously Bresson is not aiming at absolute realism. On the other hand, his stylized treatment of it does not have the pure abstract quality of a symbol. It is rather a structured presentation of the abstract and concrete, that is to say of the reciprocal interplay of seemingly incompatible elements. The rain, the murmur of a waterfall, the sound of earth pouring from a broken pot, the hooves of a horse on the cobblestones, are not there just as a contrast to the simplification of the sets or the convention of the costumes, still less as a contrast to the literary and anachronistic flavor of the dialogue. They are not needed either for dramatic antithesis or for a contrast in decor. They are there deliberately as neutrals, as foreign bodies, like a grain of sand that gets into and seizes up a piece of machinery. If the arbitrariness of their choice resembles an abstraction, it is the abstraction of the concrete integral. They are like lines drawn across an image to affirm its transparency, as the dust affirms the transparency of a diamond; it is impurity at its purest.

This interaction of sound and decor is repeated in the very midst of elements which seem at first to be completely stylized. For example, the two apartments of the women are almost totally unfurnished but this calculated bareness has its explanation. That the frames should be on the walls though the paintings have been sold is undoubtedly a deliberate touch of realism. The abstract whiteness of the new apartment is not intended as part of a pattern of theatrical expressionism. The apartment is white because it has just been repainted and the smell of fresh paint still hangs about. Is there any need to add to this list the elevator or the concierge's telephone, or, on the sound track, the tumult of male voices that follows the face-slapping of Agnes, the text for which reads totally conventionally while the sound quality of it is absolute perfection.

I have referred to *Les Dames* in discussing *Le Journal* because it is important to point out the profound similarity between the mechanics of their respective adaptations.

The style of *Le Journal* indicates a more systematic searching, a rigor that is almost unbearable. It was made under very different technical conditions. Yet we shall see that the procedure was in each case basically the same. In both it was a matter of getting to the heart of a story or of a drama, of achieving the most rigorous form of aesthetic abstraction while avoiding expressionism by way of an interplay of literature and realism, which added to its cinematic potential while seeming to negate it. In any case, Bresson's faithfulness to his model is the alibi of liberty in chains. If he is faithful to the text this is because it serves his purpose better than taking useless liberties. Furthermore, this respect for the letter is, in the last analysis, far more than an exquisite embarrassment, it is a dialectical moment in the creation of a style.

So it is pointless to complain that paradoxically Bresson is at one and the same time the slave and the master of his text because it is precisely from this seeming contradiction that he gets his effects. Henri Agel, for example, describes the film as a page of Victor Hugo rewritten in the style of de Nerval. But surely one could imagine poetic results born of this monstrous coupling, of unexpectedly revealing flashes touched off by a translation made not just from one language into another (like Mallarmé's translation of Poe) but from one style and one content into the style of another artist and from the material of one art transposed into the material of another.

Let us look a little more closely now at *Le Journal* and see what in it has not really come off. While not wishing to praise Bresson for all his weak spots, for there are weaknesses, rare ones, which work to his disadvantage, we can say quite definitely that they are all an integral part of his style; they are simply that kind of awkwardness to which a high degree of sensibility may lead, and if Bresson has any reason here for self-congratulation, it is for having had the sense to see in that awkwardness the price he must pay for something more important.

So, even if the acting in general seems poor, except for Laydu all the time and for Nicole Lamiral some of it, this, provided you like the film, will only appear to be a minor defect. But now we have to explain why Bresson who directed his cast so superbly in *Les Anges du péché* and *Les Dames du Bois de Boulogne* seems to handle them in this film as amateurishly as any tyro with a camera who has roped in his aunt and the family lawyer. Do people really imagine that it was easier to get Maria Casarès to play down her talent than to handle a group of docile amateurs? Certainly some scenes were poorly acted. It is odd however that these were by no means the least moving.

The fact is that this film is not to be measured by ordinary standards of acting. It is important to remember that the cast were all either amateurs or simple beginners. *Le Journal* no more approximates to *Ladri di Biciclette* than to *L'Entrée des artistes*. Actually the only film it can be likened to is Carl Dreyer's *Jeanne d'Arc*. The cast is not being asked to act out a text, not even to live it out, just to speak it. It is because of this that the passages spoken off-screen so perfectly match the passages spoken by the characters on-screen. There is no fundamental difference either in tone or style. This plan of attack not only rules out any dramatic interpretation by the actors but also any psychological touches either. What we are asked to look for on their faces is not for some fleeting reflection of the words but for an uninterrupted condition of soul, the outward revelation of an interior destiny.

Thus this so-called badly acted film leaves us with the feeling of having seen a gallery of portraits whose expressions could not be other than they were. In this respect the most characteristic of all is de Chantal in the confessional. Dressed in black, withdrawn into the shadows, Nicole Lamiral allows us only a glimpse of a mask, half lit, half in shadow, like a seal stamped on wax, all blurred at the edges.

Naturally Bresson, like Dreyer, is only concerned with the countenance as flesh, which, when not involved in playing a role, is a man's true imprint, the most visible mark of his soul. It is then that the countenance takes on the dignity of a sign. He would have us be concerned here not with the psychology but with the physiology of existence. Hence the hieratic tempo of the acting, the slow ambiguous gestures, the obstinate recurrence of certain behavioral patterns, the unforgettable dream-like slow motion. Nothing purely accidental could happen to these people—confirmed as each is in his own way of life, essentially concerned either against the influence of grace, to continue so, or, responding to grace, to throw off the deadly Nessus-mantle of the old Adam.

There is no development of character. Their inner conflicts, the various phases of their struggle as they wrestle with the Angel of the Lord, are never outwardly revealed. What we see is rather a concentration of suffering, the recurrent spasms of childbirth or of a snake sloughing off its skin. We can truly say that Bresson strips his characters bare.

Eschewing psychological analysis, the film in consequence lies outside the usual dramatic categories. The succession of events is not constructed according to the usual laws of dramaturgy under which the passions work towards a soul-satisfying climax. Events do indeed follow one another according to a necessary order, yet within a framework of accidental happenings. Free acts and coincidences are interwoven. Each moment in the film, each set-up, has its own due measure, alike, of freedom and of necessity. They all move in the same direction, but separately like iron filings drawn to the overall surface of a magnet. If the word tragedy comes to one's pen, it is in an opposite sense since we can only be dealing here with a tragedy freely willed. The transcendence of the Bernanos-Bresson universe is not the transcendence of destiny as the ancients understood it, nor yet the transcendence of Racinian passion, but the transcendence of grace which is something each of us is free to refuse.

If nevertheless, the concatenation of events and the causal efficiency of the characters involved appear to operate just as rigidly as in a traditional dramatic structure, it is because they are responding to an order, of prophecy (or perhaps one should say of Kirkegaardian "repetition") that is as different from fatality as causality is from analogy.

The pattern of the film's unfolding is not that of tragedy in the usual sense, rather in the sense of the medieval Passion Play, or better still, of the Way of the Cross, each sequence being a station along that road. We are given the key to this by the dialogue in the hut between the two curés, when the one from Ambricourt reveals that he is spiritually attracted to the Mount of Olives. "Is it not enough that Our Lord should have granted me the grace of letting me know today, through the words of my old teacher, that nothing, throughout all eternity, can remove me from the place chosen by me from all eternity, that I was the prisoner of His Sacred Passion?"

Death is not the preordained end of our final agony, only its conclusion and a deliverance. Henceforth we shall know to what divine ordinance, to what spiritual rhythm the sufferings and actions of the curé respond. They are the outward representation of his agony. At which point we should indicate the analogies with Christ that abound towards the end of the film, or they may very well go unnoticed. For example, the two fainting fits during the night; the fall in the mud; the vomitings of wine and blood—a remarkable synthesis of powerful comparisons with the falls of Jesus, the Blood of the Passion, the sponge with vinegar on it, and the defiling spittle. These are not all. For the veil of Veronica we have the cloth of Seraphita; then finally the death in the attic—a Golgotha with even a good and a bad thief.

Now let us immediately put aside these comparisons, the very enumeration of which is necessarily deceptive. Their aesthetic weight derives from their theological value, but both defy explanation. Bresson like Bernanos avoids any sort of symbolic allusion and so none of the situations, despite their obvious parallel to the Gospel, is created precisely because of that parallel. Each carries its own biographical and individual meaning. Its Christlike resemblance comes second, through being projected onto the higher plane of analogy. In no sense is it true to say that the life of the curé of Ambricourt is an imitation of its divine model, rather it is a repetition and a picturing forth of that life. Each bears his own cross and each cross is different, but all are the Cross of the Passion. The sweat on the brow of the curé is a bloody sweat.

So, probably for the first time, the cinema gives us a film in which the only genuine incidents, the only perceptible movements are those of the life of the spirit. Not only that, it also offers us a new dramatic form, that is specifically religious—or better still, specifically theological; a phenomenology of salvation and grace.

It is worth noting that through playing down the psychological elements and keeping the dramatics to a minimum, Bresson is left to face two kinds of pure reality. On the one hand, as we saw, we have the countenance of the actor denuded of all symbolic expression, sheer epidermis, set in a surrounding devoid of any artifice. On the other hand there is what we must call the "written reality." Indeed, Bresson's faithfulness to the text of Bernanos, his refusal, that is, not only to adapt it but also his paradoxical concern to emphasize its literary character, is part of the same predetermined approach to the direction of his actors and the selection of his settings. Bresson treats the novel as he does his characters. The novel is a cold, hard fact, a reality to be accepted as it stands. One must not attempt to adapt it to the situation in hand, or manipulate it to fit some passing need for an explanation; on the contrary it is something to be taken absolutely as it stands. Bresson never condenses the text, he cuts it. Thus what is left over is a part of the original. Like marble from a quarry the words of the film continue to be part of the novel. Of course the deliberate emphasis on their literary character can be interpreted as a search after artistic stylization, which is the very opposite of realism. The fact is, however, that in this case the reality is not the descriptive content, moral or intellectual, of the text—it is the very text itself, or more properly, the style. Clearly the reality at one stage removed of the novel and that which the camera captures directly, cannot fit or grow together or become one. On the contrary the effect of their juxtaposition is to reaffirm their differences. Each plays its part, side by side, using the means at its disposal, in its own setting and after its own style. But it is doubtless by this separating off of elements which because of their resemblance would appear to belong together, that Bresson manages to eliminate what is accidental. The ontological conflict between two orders of events, occurring simultaneously, when confronted on the screen reveal their single common measure—the soul.

Each actor says the same things and the very disparity between their expressions, the substance of what they say, their style, the kind of indifference which seems to govern the relation of actor to text, of word and visage, is the surest guarantee of their close complicity. This language which no lips could speak is, of necessity, from the soul.

It is unlikely that there exists anywhere in the whole of French cinema, perhaps even in all French literature, many moments of a more intense beauty than in the medallion scene between the curé and the countess. Its beauty does not derive from the acting nor from the psychological and dramatic values of the dialogue, nor indeed from its intrinsic meaning. The true dialogue that punctuates the struggle between the inspired priest and a soul in despair is, of its very nature, ineffable. The decisive clashes of their spiritual fencing-match escape us. Their words announce, or prepare the way for, the fiery touch of grace. There is nothing here then of the flow of words that usually goes with a conversion, while the overpowering severity of the dialogue, its rising tension and its final calm leave us with the conviction that we have been the privileged witnesses of a supernatural storm. The words themselves are so much dead weight, the echo of a silence that is the true dialogue between these two souls; a hint at their secret; the opposite side of the coin, if one dare to say so, of the Divine Countenance. When later the curé refuses to come to his own defense by producing the countess' letter, it is not out of humility or love of suffering. It is rather because no tangible evidence is worthy to play a part either in his defense or his indictment. Of its nature the evidence of the countess is no more acceptable than that of de Chantal, and none has the right to ask God to bear witness.

The technique of Bresson's direction cannot adequately be judged except at the level of his aesthetic intention. Inadequately as we may have so far described the latter, it may yet be that the highly astonishing paradox of the film is now a little more evident. Actually the distinction of having set text over against image for the first time goes to Melville in his *Silence de la mer*. It is noteworthy that his reason was likewise a desire for fidelity. However, the structure of Vercors' book was of itself unusual. In his *Journal* Bresson has done more than justify Melville's experiment and shown how well warranted it was. He has carried it to its final conclusions.

Is *Le Journal* just a silent film with spoken titles? The spoken word, as we have seen, does not enter into the image as a realistic component. Even when spoken by one of the characters, it rather resembles the recitative of an opera. At first sight the film seems to be somehow made up on the one hand of the abbreviated text of the novel and illustrated, on the other hand, by images that never pretend to replace it. All that is spoken is not seen, yet nothing that is seen but is also spoken. At worst, critical good sense can reproach Bresson with having substituted an illustrated radiophonic montage, no less, for Bernanos' novel.

So it is from this ostensible corruption of the art of cinema that we begin if we are to grasp fully Bresson's originality and boldness.

In the first place, if Bresson "returns" to the silent film it is certainly not, despite the abundance of close-ups, because he wants to tie in again with theatrical expressionism—that fruit of an infirmity—on the contrary, it is in order to rediscover the dignity of the human countenance as understood by Stroheim and Dreyer. Now if there is one and only one quality of the silent film irreconcilable of its very nature with sound, it is the syntactical subtlety of montage and expression in the playing of the film, that is to say that which proceeds in effect from the weakness of the silent film. But not all silent films want to be such. Nostalgia for a silence that would be the benign procreator of a visual symbolism unduly confuses the so-called primacy of the image with the true vocation of the cinema—which is the primacy of the object. The absence of a sound track for *Greed, Nosferatu,* or *La Passion de Jeanne d'Arc* means something quite other than the silence of *Caligari, Die Nibelungen,* or *Eldorado.* It is a frustration not the foundation of a form of expression. The former films exist in spite of their silence not because of it. In this sense the invention of the sound track is just a fortuitous scientific phenomenon and not the aesthetic revolution people always say it is. The language of film, like the language of Aesop, is ambiguous and in spite of appearances to the contrary, the history of cinema before and after 1928 is an unbroken continuity. It is the story of the relations between expressionism and realism. Sound was to destroy expressionism for a while before adopting it in its turn. On the other hand, it became an immediate part of the continued development of realism.

Paradoxically enough it is to the most theatrical, that is to say to the most talkative, forms of the sound film that we must look today for a resurgence of the old symbolism while the pre-talkie realism of a Stroheim has in fact no following. Yet, it is evident that Bresson's undertaking is somehow related to the work of Stroheim and Renoir. The separating of sound and of the image to which it relates cannot be understood without a searching examination of the aesthetics of realism in sound. It is just as mistaken to see it as an illustration of a text, as a commentary on an image. Their parallelism maintains that division which is present to our senses. It continues the Bressonian dialectic between abstraction and reality thanks to which we are concerned with a single reality—that of human souls. In no sense does Bresson return to the expressionism of the silent film. On the one hand he excludes one of the components of reality in order to reproduce it, deliberately stylized on a sound track, partially independent of the image. In other words, it is as if the final rerecording was composed of sound directly recorded with scrupulous fidelity and a text postsynchronized on a monotone. But, as we have pointed out, this text is itself a second

139

reality, a "cold aesthetic fact." Its realism is its style, while the style of the image is primarily its reality, and the style of the film is precisely the conflict between the two.

Bresson disposes once and for all of that commonplace of criticism according to which image and sound should never duplicate one another. The most moving moments in the film are those in which text and image are saying the same thing, each however in its own way. The sound never serves simply to fill out what we see. It strengthens it and multiplies it just as the echo chamber of a violin echoes and multiplies the vibrations of the strings. Yet this metaphor is dialectically inadequate since it is not so much a resonance that the mind perceives as something that does not match, as when a color is not properly superimposed on a drawing. It is here at the edge that the event reveals its true significance. It is because the film is entirely structured on this relationship that, towards the end, the images take on such emotional power. It would be in vain to look for its devastating beauty simply in what is explicit. I doubt if the individual frames in any other film, taken separately, are so deceptive. Their frequent lack of plastic composition, the awkwardness and static quality of the actors completely mislead one as to their value in the overall film. Moreover, this accretion of effectiveness is not due to the editing. The value of an image does not depend on what precedes or follows it. They accumulate, rather, a static energy, like the parallel leaves of a condenser. Between this and the sound track differences of aesthetic potential are set up, the tension of which becomes unbearable. Thus the image-text relationship moves towards its climax, the latter having the advantage. Thus it is that, quite naturally, at the command of an imperious logic, there is nothing more that the image has to communicate except by disappearing. The spectator has been led, step by step, towards that night of the senses the only expression of which is a light on a blank screen.

That is where the so-called silent film and its lofty realism is headed, to the disappearance of the image and its replacement simply by the text of the novel. But here we are experimenting with an irrefutable aesthetic, with a sublime achievement of pure cinema. Just as the blank page of Mallarmé and the silence of Rimbaud is language at the highest state, the screen, free of images and handed back to literature, is the triumph of cinematographic realism. The black cross on the white screen, as awkwardly drawn as on the average memorial card, the only trace left by the "assumption" of the image, is a witness to something the reality of which is itself but a sign.

With *Le Journal* cinematographic adaptation reaches a new stage. Up to now, film tended to substitute for the novel in the guise of its aesthetic translation into another language. Fidelity meant respect for the spirit of the novel, but it also meant a search for necessary equivalents, that is to say, it meant taking into account the dramatic requirements of the theater or again the more direct effectiveness of the cinematographic image. Unfortunately, concern for these things will continue to be the general rule. We must remember however that it was through their application that *Le Diable au corps* and *La Symphonie pastorale* turned out so well. According to the best opinions, films like these are as good as the books on which they are modelled.

In the margin of this formula we might also note the existence of the free adaptation of books such as that made by Renoir for *Une Partie de campagne* or *Madame Bovary*. Here the problem is solved in another way. The original is just a source of inspiration. Fidelity is here the temperamental affinity between film-maker and novelist, a deeply sympathetic understanding. Instead of presenting itself as a substitute, the film is intended to take its place alongside the book—to make a pair with it, like twin stars. This assumption, applicable only where there is genius, does not exclude the possibility that the film is a greater achievement than its literary model, as in the case of Renoir's *The River*.

Le Journal however is something else again. Its dialectic between fidelity and creation is reducible, in the last analysis, to a dialectic between the cinema and literature. There is no question here of a translation, no matter how faithful or intelligent. Still less is it a question of free inspiration with the intention of making a duplicate. It is a question of building a secondary work with the novel as foundation. In no sense is the film "comparable" to the novel or "worthy" of it. It is a new aesthetic creation, the novel so to speak multiplied by the cinema.

The only procedure in any way comparable of which we have any examples are films of paintings. Emmer or Alain Resnais are similarly faithful to the original, their raw material is the already highly developed work of the painter; the reality with which they are concerned is not the subject of the painting but the painting itself, in the same way as the text of the novel is Bresson's reality. But the fidelity of Alain Resnais to Van Gogh is but the prior condition of a symbiosis of cinema and painting. That is why, as a rule, painters fail utterly to understand the whole procedure. If you see these films as nothing more than an intelligent, effective, and even a valuable means of popularizing painting—they certainly are that too—you know nothing of their aesthetic biology.

This comparison with films of paintings, however, is only partially valid since these are confined from the outset to the realm of minor aesthetic works. They add something to the paintings, they prolong their existence, they release them from the confines of their frames but they can never pretend to be the paintings themselves.* The Van Gogh of Alain Resnais is a minor masterpiece taken from a major work which it makes use of and explains in detail but does not replace. There are two reasons for this congenital limitation. First of all, the photographic reproduction, in projection, cannot pretend to be a substitute for the original or to share its identity. If it could, then it would be the better to destroy its aesthetic autonomy, since films of paintings start off precisely as the negation of

---

* At least up to the time of *Le Mystère Picasso* which, as we shall see, may invalidate this criticism.

that on which this aesthetic autonomy is based, the fact that the paintings are circumscribed in space and exist outside time. It is because cinema as the art of space and time is the contrary of painting that it has something to add to it.

Such a contradiction does not exist between the novel and the film. Not only are they both narrative arts, that is to say temporal arts, but it is not even possible to maintain a priori that the cinematic image is essentially inferior to the image prompted by the written word. In all probability the opposite is the case. But this is not where the problem lies. It is enough if the novelist, like the filmmaker, is concerned with the idea of unfolding a real world. Once we accept these essential resemblances, there is nothing absurd in trying to write a novel on film. But *Le Journal* has just proved to us that it is more fruitful to speculate on their differences rather than on their resemblances, that is, for the existence of the novel to be affirmed by the film and not dissolved into it. It is hardly enough to say of this work, once removed, that it is in essence faithful to the original because, to begin with, it *is* the novel. But most of all the resulting work is not, certainly, better (that kind of judgment is meaningless . . .) but "more" than the book. The aesthetic pleasure we derive from Bresson's film, while the acknowledgment for it goes, essentially, to the genius of Bernanos, includes all that the novel has to offer plus, in addition, its refraction in the cinema.

After Bresson, Aurenche and Bost are but the Viollet-le-Duc of cinematographic adaptation.

CHARLIE CHAPLIN

Charlie is a Mythical Character

Charlie is a mythical figure who rises above every adventure in which he becomes involved. For the general public, Charlie exists as a person before and after *Easy Street* and *The Pilgrim*. For hundreds of millions of people on this planet he is a hero like Ulysses or Roland in other civilizations—but with the difference that we know the heroes of old through literary works that are complete and have defined once and for all, their adventures and their various manifestations. Charlie, on the other hand, is always free to appear in another film. The living Charlie remains the creator and guarantor of Charlie the character.

But What Makes Charlie Run?

But the continuity and coherence of Charlie's aesthetic existence can only be experienced by way of the films that he inhabits. The public recognizes him from his face and especially from his little trapezoidal moustache and his duck-like waddle rather than from his dress which, here again, does not make the monk. In *The Pil-*

144

grim we see him dressed only as a convict and as a clergyman and in a lot of films he wears a tuxedo or the elegant cutaway coat of a millionaire. These physical "markings" would be of less than no importance if one did not perceive, more importantly, the interior constants that are the true constituents of the character. These are however less easy to define or describe. One way would be to examine his reaction to a particular event, for example his complete absence of obstinacy when the world offers too strong an opposition. In such cases he tries to get round the problem rather than solve it. A temporary way out is enough for him, just as if for him there was no such thing as the future. For example in *The Pilgrim* he props a rolling-pin on a shelf with a bottle of milk that he is going to need in a minute or two. Of course the rolling-pin falls onto his head. While a provisional solution always seems to satisfy him he shows a fabulous ingenuity in the immediate circumstance. He is never at a loss in any situation. There is a solution for everything even though the world (and especially things in it rather than the people) is not made for him.

Charlie and Things

The utilitarian function of things relates to a human order of things itself utilitarian and which in turn has an eye to the future. In our world, things are tools, some more some less efficient, but all directed towards a specific purpose. However, they do not serve Charlie as they serve us. Just as human society never accepts him even provisionally except as a result of a misunderstanding, every time that Charlie wants to use something for the purpose for which it was made, that is to say, within the framework of our society, either he goes about it in an extremely awkward fashion (especially at table) or the things themselves refuse to be used, almost it would seem deliberately. In *A Day's Pleasure* the engine of the old Ford

145

stops every time he opens the door. In *One A.M.* his bed moves around unpredictably so that he cannot lie down. In *The Pawnshop* the works of the alarm clock that he had just taken to pieces start moving around on their own like worms. But, conversely, things which refuse to serve him the way they serve us are in fact used by him to much better purpose because he puts them to multifarious uses according to his need at the moment.

The street lamp in *Easy Street* serves the function of an anaesthetist's mask to asphyxiate the terror of the neighborhood. A little later a cast-iron stove is used to knock the man flat, whereas the "functional" truncheon only gives him a slight singing in the ears. In *The Adventurer* a blind transforms him into a lampstand, invisible to the police. In *Sunnyside* a shirt serves as a tablecloth, as sleeves, as a towel, and so on. It looks as if things are only willing to be of use to him in ways that are purely marginal to the uses assigned by society. The most beautiful example of these strange uses is the famous dance of the rolls which contribute to a sudden outburst of highly unusual choreography.

Let us look at another characteristic gag. In *The Adventurer* Charlie thinks he has disposed of the warders pursuing him, by pelting them with stones from the top of a cliff. The warders are actually lying on the ground more or less unconscious. Instead of seizing the opportunity to put daylight between himself and them, he amuses himself by throwing more stones, pebbles this time, by way of refining on the operation. While he is doing this he fails to notice that another warder has arrived behind him and is watching him. As he reaches for another stone his hand touches the warden's shoe. His reaction is something to marvel at. Instead of trying to run away, which would in any case be useless, or having sized up his desperate plight, handing himself over to the officer, Charlie covers the ill-met shoe with a handful of dust. You laugh and your neighbor laughs too. At first it is all the same laughter. But I have "listened in" to this gag twenty times in different theaters. When the audience, or at least part of it, was made up of intellectuals, students for example, there was a second wave of laughter of a different kind. At that moment the hall was no longer filled with the original laughter but with a series of echoes, a second wave of laughter, reflected off the minds of the spectators as if from the invisible walls of an abyss. These echoed effects are not always audible; first of all they depend on the audience but most of all because Charlie's gags are often of such short duration that they allow just enough time for you to "get it," nor are they followed by a time lag that gives you a chance to think about them. It is the opposite of the technique called for in the theater by the laughter from the house. Although he was brought up in the school of the music hall, Charlie has refined down its comedy, refusing in any way to pander to the public. This need for simplicity and effectiveness requires of the gag the greatest elliptical clarity, and once he has achieved this he refuses to elaborate on it.

The technique of Charlie's gags naturally calls for a study to itself, which we cannot undertake here. Sufficient perhaps that we have made it clear that they have attained a kind of final perfection, the highest degree of style. It is stupid to treat Charlie as a clown of genius. If there had never been a cinema he would undoubtedly have been a clown of genius, but the cinema has allowed him to raise the comedy of circus and music hall to the highest aesthetic level. Chaplin needed the medium of the cinema to free comedy completely from the limits of space and time imposed by the stage or the circus arena.

Thanks to the camera, the evolution of the comic effect which is being presented, all the while with the greatest clarity, not only does not need boosting so that a whole audience can enjoy it, on the contrary it can now be refined down to the utmost degree; thus the machinery is kept to a minimum, so that it becomes a high-precision mechanism capable of responding instantly to the most delicate of springs.

It is significant, furthermore, that the best Chaplin films can be seen over and over again with no loss of pleasure—indeed the very opposite is the case. It is doubtless a fact that the satisfaction derived from certain gags is inexhaustible, so deep does it lie, but it is furthermore supremely true that comic form and aesthetic value owe nothing to surprise. The latter is exhausted the first time around and is replaced by a much more subtle pleasure, namely the delight of anticipating and recognizing perfection.

Charlie and Time

Whatever the facts, one can clearly see that the gag referred to above opens up under the initial comic shock a spiritual abyss which induces in the spectator, without giving him a chance to analyze it, that delicious vertigo that quickly modifies the tone of the laughter it provokes. The reason is that Charlie carries to absurd lengths his basic principle of never going beyond the actual moment. Having got rid of his two wardens, thanks to his capacity to exploit the terrain and whatever objects are to hand, once the danger is past he immediately stops thinking about building up a reserve store of supplementary prudence. The consequence is not long delayed. But this time it is so serious that Charlie is not able to find an immediate solution—rest assured that he soon will—he cannot go beyond a reflex action and the pretence at improvisation. One second, just time enough for a gesture of dismissal and the threat, in illusion, will have been effaced by the derisory stroke of an eraser. Let no one, however, stupidly confuse Charlie's gesture with that of an ostrich burying its head in the sand. The whole bearing of Charlie refutes this; it is sheer improvisation, unlimited imagination in the face of danger. The swiftness of the threat, however, and above all its brutal nature in contrast to the euphorious condition of the mind in which it takes conscious shape, does not allow him, this time, to escape immediately. Besides who can tell—because of the surprise it gives to the warden who was expecting a gesture of fear—if his action will not in the end allow him that fraction of a second that he needs to make his escape? Instead of solving the problem Charlie has no recourse other than to pretend things are not what they seem.

As a matter of fact this gesture of brushing aside danger is one of a number of gags peculiar to Charlie. Among these should be included the celebrated occasion when he camouflages himself as a tree in *Shoulder Arms*. "Camouflage" is not really the right term. It is more properly a form of mimicry. One might go so far as to say that the defense reflexes of Charlie end in a reabsorption of time by space. Driven into a corner by a terrible and unavoidable danger, Charlie hides behind appearances like a crab burying itself in the sand. And this is no mere metaphor. At the opening of *The Adventurer* we see the convict emerging from the sand in which he was hiding, and burying himself again when danger returns.

The painted canvas tree in which Charlie is hiding blends in with the trees of the forest in a way that is quite "hallucinating." One is reminded of those little stick-like insects that are indiscernible in a clump of twigs or those little Indian insects that can take on the appearance of leaves, even leaves that caterpillars have nibbled. The sudden vegetable-like immobility of Charlie-the-tree is like an insect playing dead, as is his other gag in *The Adventurer* when he pretends to have been killed by a shot from a warden's gun. But what distinguishes Charlie from the insect is the speed with which he returns from his condition of spatial dissolution into the cosmos, to a state of instant readiness for action. Thus, motionless inside his tree he flattens out, one after the other, with swift precise movements of his "branches," a file of German soldiers as they come within range.

The Swift Kick Characterizes the Man

It is with a simple and yet sublime gesture that Charlie expresses his supreme detachment from that biographical and social world in which we are plunged and which, for us, is a cause for regret and uneasiness, namely that remarkable backward kick which he employs to dispose alike of a banana peel, the head of Goliath and, more ideally still, of every bothersome thought. It is significant that Charlie never kicks straight ahead. Even when he kicks his partners in the pants he manages to do it while looking the other way. A cobbler would explain that this was because of the points of his outsize shoes. However, perhaps I may be allowed to ignore this piece of superficial realism and to see in the style and frequent and very personal use of this backward kick the reflection of a very vital approach to things. On the other hand, Charlie never liked, if I may dare to say so, to approach a problem head on. He prefers to take it by surprise with his back turned. On the other hand, especially when it seems to have no precise purpose, a simple gesture of revenge for example, this back-kick is a perfect expression of his constant determination not to be attached to the past, not to drag anything along behind him. This admirable gesture is furthermore capable of a thousand nuances ranging all the way from peevish revenge to a gay "I'm free at last," except, that is to say, when he is not shaking off an invisible thread attached to his leg.

The Sin of Repetition

His use of the mechanical is the price he is forced to pay for his nonadherence to the normal sequence of events and to the function of things. Since for him things have no future in the sense of being planned to serve an end, when Charlie is involved with an object for some time he quickly contracts a sort of mechanical cramp, a surface condition in which the original reason for what he is doing is forgotten. This unfortunate inclination always serves him well. It is the basis for the famous gag in *Modern Times* when Charlie, working on the assembly line, continues spasmodically to tighten imaginary bolts; in *Easy Street,* we observe it in a more subtle form. When the big tough is chasing him round the room Charlie shoves the bed between them. There then follows a series of feints in the course of which each moves up and down his side of the bed. After a while, in spite of the continued danger, Charlie becomes used to this temporary defense tactic, and instead of continuing to direct his movements by the movements of his adversary, ends by running up and down on his own side as if the gesture were sufficient of itself to ward off all danger forever. Naturally, no matter how stupid the other man might be, all he has to do is to switch rhythm, to have Charlie run right into his arms. I am confident that in all Charlie's pictures there is not one where this mechanical movement does not end badly for him. In other words, mechanization of movement is in a sense Charlie's original sin, the ceaseless temptation. His independence of things and events can only be projected in time in the shape of something mechanical, like a force of inertia which continues under its initial impetus. The activity of a social being, such as you or I, is planned with foresight and as it develops, its direction is checked by constant reference to the reality that it is concerned to shape. It adheres throughout to the evolution of the event of which it is becoming part. Charlie's activity on the contrary is composed of a succession of separate instants sufficient to each of which is the evil thereof. Then laziness supervenes and Charlie continues thereafter to offer the solution proper to a previous and specific moment. The capital sin of Charlie, and he does not hesitate to make us laugh about it at his own expense, is to project into time a mode of being that is suited to one instant, and that is what is meant by "repetition."

I think we should also include in this sin of repetition the category of well-known gags in which we see a joyous Charlie brought to order by reality, for example the famous gag in *Modern Times* when he wants to bathe and dives into a river that is little more than a foot deep or again, at the beginning of *Easy Street* when, converted by love, he walks out of a room and falls on his face on the stairway. Subject to a more precise check, I would be willing to suggest that every time Charlie makes us laugh at his own expense and not at that of other people, it is when he has been imprudent enough, one way or another, to presume that the future will resemble the past or to join naively in the game as played by society and to have faith in its elaborate machinery for buildng the future . . . its moral, religious, social and political machinery.

A Man beyond the Realm of the Sacred

One of the most characteristic aspects of Charlie's freedom in respect to the demands of society is his total indifference to the category of things held sacred. Naturally by sacred I here mean, first of all, the various social aspects of the religious life. Charlie's old films add up to the most formidable anticlerical indictment imaginable of provincial puritan society in the United States. One has only to recall *The Pilgrim* and the incredible faces of those deacons, sacristans, and sharp-featured, toothy, bigoted females, the solemn and angular Quakers. The world of Dubout is a world of child's play alongside this social caricature worthy of Daumier. But the principal strength of this portrait derives from the fact that the acid which has etched this engraving is in no sense anticlericalism. It is rather what ought to be called a radical a-clericism, and this keeps the film within the bounds of what is acceptable. There is no sacrilegious intent. No clergyman could take offense at Charlie's outfit. But there is something worse here, namely a sort of nullifying of whatever justification there is for such people, their beliefs and their behavior. Charlie has absolutely nothing against them. He can even pretend to go through the Sunday ritual, to pantomime the sermon for their pleasure or to remove the suspicions of the police. It is almost as if he had introduced a Negro dance into the ritual. In one blow, ritual and faithful are relegated to a world of the absurd, reduced to the condition of ridiculous, even of obscene objects, by being deprived of all meaning. By way of a derisory paradox the only actions throughout the ceremony that make any sense are in fact Charlie's gestures when he tests the weight of the collection-bag, rewarding the generous with a smile and the mean with a frown. Another example is the way he returns several times after his sermon to bow to his audience like a contented vaudeville actor. Nor is it a matter of chance that the one spectator who enters into the game and applauds is a snotty-nosed urchin who has spent the entire service, in spite of his mother's remonstrances, fly-watching.

However, there are other rituals besides the religious. Society approves a thousand forms of acceptable behavior which are a sort of permanent liturgy that it performs in its own honor. This is particularly true of table manners. Charlie never really manages to master the use of his knife and fork. He regularly gets his elbow among the plates, spills his soup on his pants and so on. The high spot surely is when he is himself a waiter, as in *The Rink*. Religious or not, the sacred is everywhere present in the life of society and not only in the magistrate, the policeman, the priest, but in the ritual associated with eating, with professional relations, and public transportation. It is the way that society retains its cohesion as if within a magnetic field. Unknowingly, every minute of our time we adjust to this framework. But Charlie is of another metal. Not only does he elude its grasp, but the very category of the sacred does not exist for him. Such a thing is, to him, as inconceivable as the color of a pink geranium is to someone born blind.

To put it more precisely, a good part of Charlie's comedy is born of the efforts he makes (to fit the needs of a temporary situation) to imitate us, as for example when he forces himself to eat politely, even with delicacy, or when he adds a touch of derisive coquetry to his dress.

CINEMA AND EXPLORATION

IN HIS little book *Le Cinéma au long cours (Filming in Far-Off Lands)*, Jean Thévenot has traced the development of the film of exploration from its successful beginnings, around 1928, through the period of its decline, between 1930 and 1940, to its rebirth following World War II. The implications of this evolution are worth studying.

It was after World War I, that is to say in 1920, some ten years after it was filmed by Ponting during the heroic expedition of Scott to the South Pole, that *With Scott to the South Pole* revealed to the film-going public those polar landscapes which were to constitute the major success of a series of films of which Flaherty's *Nanook* (1922) is still the outstanding example. Not long afterwards, very likely because of the success of the Arctic films, a type of production appeared which we might categorize as "tropical and equatorial." The best known are those filmed in Africa, and in particular *La Croisière Noire* by Leon Poirier, *Cimbo,* and *Congorilla*—the first dating from 1926, and the last two filmed between 1923 and 1927, but only shown publicly in 1928. In these first travel-films-in-the-grand-manner we already see what are the chief values of this category: an authentically poetic quality which does not age and is admirably exemplified in *Nanook*. But this poetry, especially in those films shot in the South Seas, began to take on an exotic quality. From *Moana,* virtually an ethnographic document, to *Tabu,* by way of *White Shadows,* we are aware of the gradual formation of a mythology. We see the Western mind as it were taking over a far-off civilization and interpreting it after its own fashion.

In French literature those were the days of Paul Morand, of Mac Orlan, and of Blaise Cendrars. The new mystique of the exotic, given a new life by the new media of communication, and which one might reasonably call "instant exoticism," was most typically expressed in a film made in the early days of sound. It flung the whole earth onto the screen in a jigsaw of visual images and sounds and was entitled *Melodie der Welt.* Made by Walther Ruttmann, it was one of the initial successes of a new art form.

Thenceforward, with a few outstanding exceptions, the exotic film went into a decline characterized by a shameless search after the spectacular and the sensational. It was not enough merely to hunt the lion, the lion must first gobble up the bearers. In *L'Afrique vous parle* a Negro gets eaten by a crocodile. In *Trader Horn* another Negro is charged by a rhinoceros. On this occasion the chase appeared to be staged, but the same intention was clearly there. Thus there came into existence the myth of an Africa inhabited by savages and wild beasts, the culmination of which was *Tarzan* and *King Solomon's Mines.*

Since World War II we have witnessed a definite return to documentary authenticity. The cycle of exoticism reached its climax in absurdity. Today the public demands that what it sees shall be believable, a faith that can be tested by the other media of information, namely, radio, books, and the daily press.

The rebirth of the film of exploration is basically due to a renewed interest in exploration, the mystique of which may very well turn out to be something quite other than the old exoticism as may be seen for example in *Rendez-vous de juillet.*

It is this new point of departure which gives to the present expeditions their style and their direction. These derive in the first place from the character of today's exploration which is for the most part either scientific or anthropological. While sensationalism is not absolutely excluded it is nevertheless subordinated to the objectively documentary purpose of the expedition. The result is that the sensational is virtually eliminated, for it is rarely possible, as we shall see, for the camera to be a witness to the most dangerous moments of an expedition. By way of compensation, the psychological and human elements move into the foreground. There are two occasions when this is particularly true. The first is when the behavior of the members of the expedition and their reactions to the task in hand constitute a kind of anthropology of an explorer, the experimental psychology as it were of an adventurer. The second is when the people under study are no longer treated as a species of exotic animal, and who perforce must be fully described so that they may be better understood.

Furthermore the film is no longer the only, nor even probably the principal instrument for bringing the realities of the expedition before the public. Today it is usually accompanied by a book or shown during a series of lectures, first at the Salle Pleyel, then in a few scattered cities throughout France. These will be followed by radio and television versions. And all of this for the very good reason that, economics aside, a film cannot cover every aim of an expedition, not even its principal material aspects. Besides, this type of film is conceived as an illustrated lecture, where the presence and the words of the speaker-witness constantly complement and authenticate the image on the screen.

At which point let me cite a film that runs counter to this evolutionary trend and furthermore is proof enough that the documentary-film-by-reconstruction is dead. The film in question is an English Technicolor film, *Scott of the Antarctic,* the French title of which is *L'Aventure sans retour,* which retells the story of the expedition of Captain Scott in 1911 and 1912. It is ostensibly the very expedition shown in *With Scott to the South Pole.*

Let us first recall the heroic and moving character of this undertaking. Scott set out to conquer the South Pole with revolutionary but as yet experimental equipment; a few "caterpillars," some ponies, and dogs. The machines were the first to let him down. Then by degrees the ponies died of exhaustion. By now there were not enough dogs to serve the needs of the expedition and the five men on the final stage from their last camp to the Pole were obliged to pull their own supply sledges, a round trip estimated at approximately 1250 miles. They reached their objective only to find that Amundsen had planted the Norwegian flag there a few hours before. The return trip was one long agony; the last three survivors, the oil for their lamps exhausted, froze to death in their tents. Three months later, their comrades from the base camp found them and were able to reconstruct their Odyssey, thanks to a diary kept by the leader and to some exposed photographic plates.

This undertaking of Captain Scott marks perhaps the first, albeit unfortunate, attempt at a modern scientific expedition. Scott failed where Amundsen succeeded because he tried to do something outside the established and well-tried techniques of a polar expedition. Nevertheless his unfortunate "caterpillars" are the forerunners of the "Weasels" used by Paul-Emile Victor and Liotard. It also provides the first example of a practice which is now common, namely, the provision for a cinematic report as an integral part of the expedition itself. Their cameraman, Ponting, whose film was the first ever to be made of a Polar expedition, had his hands frostbitten while reloading without gloves in a temperature of $-30°C$. While Ponting did not accompany Scott on the long trek to the pole, his film of the voyage south, of the preparations for the expedition, of life at the base camp, and of the tragic ending of the expedition remain at once a moving testimony to the adventure, and the archetype of all films of this genre.

England is understandably proud of Captain Scott and would naturally want to pay tribute to him. Yet, for my part I have never seen a more boring and ridiculous undertaking than *Scott of the*

157

Antarctic. Here is a film so lavishly and carefully made that it must have cost as much as the original expedition. Considering the time at which it was made, 1947–1948, it is also a Technicolor masterpiece. The studio reconstructions reveal a mastery of trick work and studio imitation—but to what purpose? To imitate the inimitable, to reconstruct that which of its very nature can only occur once, namely risk, adventure, death. Certainly the scenario is no help. Scott's life and death are told with an almost pedantic formality. I will not dwell on the moral of the story, which is nothing but a Boy Scout moral raised to the dignity of a national institution. The real failure of the film does not lie there, but in its out-of-date technique, and for two reasons.

First of all the film takes no account of the scientific information concerning polar exploration which the man in the street now has at his command. He derives this competence from newspaper reports, from radio, television, and cinema. To draw a parallel in educational terms, one might say of this film that it offers scientific information on a grammar-school level to high-school graduates. This is unfortunate, when the aim is an educational one. Admittedly Scott's expedition was indeed one rather of exploration, its scientific aspect being little more than tentative, and as it turned out, unsuccessful. For this very reason the producers should have been concerned to explain at greater length the psychological context of the adventure. To anyone seeing *Greenland* by Marcel Ichac and Languepin at the cinema across the way, Scott would appear an obstinate fool. Admittedly the director, Charles Frend, took pains in a number of unfortunately heavily didactic scenes to describe the social, moral, and technical surroundings out of which the expedition was born, but he does so for an England of 1910. What he should have done by way of some storytelling device or other was to draw a parallel with our own times, because this is what the audience will instinctively do. Secondly, and this most importantly, the prevalence of objective reporting following World War II defined once and for all what it is that we require from such reports.

Exoticism with all its romantic and spectacular seduction has given way to a taste for the critical handling of the facts for their own sake. Ponting's film of the expedition is ancestor to both *Kon Tiki* and *Greenland,* that is to say to the shortcomings of the one and to the determination to make an exhaustive report evident in the other.

The simple snapshot of Scott and his four companions at the pole, which was discovered in their baggage, is far more stirring than the entire Technicolor feature by Charles Frend.

The extent to which his film is a pointless undertaking is even more evident when one discovers that it was made among the glaciers of Norway and Switzerland. The realization that these settings, although they may bear some resemblance to the Antarctic, are nevertheless not the Antarctic, is enough of itself to destroy any sense of drama with which the subject would otherwise be charged. If I had been in Charles Frend's position I would have done my best to include some shots from the Ponting film. It would be just a matter of planning the scenario. Thus by including some of the stark realities of the original, the film would have taken on a meaning which it now completely lacks.

By comparison, what Marcel Ichac and Languepin brought back in *Greenland* can be considered as an example of one of the two contrasting forms assumed by records of contemporary expeditions, of which *With Scott to the South Pole* is the forebear. The preparations for P.-E. Victor's expedition took into account, doubtless, certain likely risks but tried to anticipate them as far as possible. Cinematography was added as a supplementary special service. Strictly speaking the sequence of the film could have been planned before the expedition set out as were the day-to-day activities of the members of the expedition. The director in any case was free to use his equipment as he saw fit. He was there as an official witness, so to speak, along with the meteorologist or geologist.

The film by Thor Heyerdahl on the other hand is an example of another kind of reporting, where the film is not an integral part of the expedition. *Kon Tiki* manages to be the most beautiful of films while not being a film at all. Like those moss-covered stones that, surviving, allow us to reconstruct buildings and statues that no longer exist, the pictures that are here presented are the remains of an unfinished creation about which one hardly dares to dream. Let me explain. Most people are familiar with the extraordinary adventures of a small group of young Norwegian and Swedish scientists who had decided to prove that, contrary to the general theory, Polynesia might well have been populated by sea migrations from certain parts of the Peruvian coast. The best way to prove their point was for them to simulate the operation as it might have been carried out thousands of years ago. Our amateur navigators constructed a sort of raft from the oldest documentary information they could find on the methods employed by the Indians themselves. The raft, not being provided with any method of steering, drifted like flotsam and was carried along by the trade winds to the Polynesian atolls, a distance of approximately 4500 miles. That this fabulous expedition should have succeeded after three solitary months and in the teeth of half a dozen storms is something to rejoice the spirit, and to be inscribed among present-day miracles. It reminds one of Melville and Conrad. The travellers brought back from their journey a book of the highest interest and a collection of delightfully humorous drawings. Nevertheless, it was evident already by 1952 that there could be no witness to the stature of the enterprise comparable to the movie camera. It is precisely this fact that provides the critic with food for reflection.

Our friends did have a camera. But they were amateurs. Their knowledge of how to handle it was no better than yours or mine. Besides they had clearly no intention of putting their film to a commercial use—as certain unhappy facts prove. For example, they operated their camera at silent speed, that is to say at 16 frames per second, while sound projection calls for 24 frames per second. The result was that every other frame had to be duplicated and the film in consequence is more jerky than the projection in provincial cinemas back in 1910. Furthermore the quality of the film is not helped by errors of exposure and by the subsequent enlargement to 35mm.

But this is by no means the worst of it. In no sense was the making of a film, even as a sideline, an integral part of the enterprise, while the shooting conditions were as bad as they could possibly be. What I mean by this is that as he lay there curled up on the edge of the raft at sea level, it was as if the cameraman, whoever he chanced to be, and the camera were simply of a piece. Naturally enough, there could be no travelling shots, no dolly shots, and scarcely a chance to get a full shot of the "vessel" from the little rubber boat bouncing on the waves astern. Finally, and most important of all, whenever something of significance occurred, the onset of a storm for example, the crew were too busy to bother about running a camera. The result was that our amateur film-makers simply wasted endless reels filming their pet parrot and the rations provided by the American armed forces. But when an exciting moment arrives, say a whale hurling itself at the raft, the footage is so short that you have to process it ten times over in the optical printer before you can even spot what is happening.

Yet somehow *Kon Tiki* is an admirable and overwhelming film. Why? Because the making of it is so totally identified with the action that it so imperfectly unfolds; because it is itself an aspect of the adventure. Those fluid and trembling images are as it were the objectivized memory of the actors in the drama. Does the killer whale, that we can barely see refracted in the water, interest us because of the rarity of the beast and of the glimpse we get of it, slight as it is? Or rather is it because the shot was taken at the very moment when a capricious movement of the monster might well have annihilated the raft and sent camera and cameraman seven or eight thousand meters into the deep? The answer is clear. It is not so much the photograph of the whale that interests us as the photograph of the *danger*. Nevertheless, the fact remains that we can

161

never feel truly satisfied with just the premature ruins of a film that was never completed. One is thus set dreaming of the photographic splendor of the films of Flaherty. Think, for example, of the shots of the basking sharks of *Man of Aran* floating drowsily on the Irish waters. But if we reflect a little further we find ourselves caught inextricably in a dilemma. What we see is not after all as imperfect as all that, and for the reason that it does not falsify the conditions of the experience it recounts. For a film in 35mm with operating room enough to make a coherently edited work it would have been necessary to build a different kind of raft, and to make it—why not—a boat like any other. But the fauna of the Pacific nudging at the raft was there precisely because it had all the characteristics of flotsam. An engine and propeller would have put them to flight. A marine paradise instantly destroyed by science! The fact of the matter is that this kind of film can actually achieve a more or less successful compromise between the exigencies of the action and the demands of reporting. A cinematographic witness to an event is what a man can seize of it on film while at the same time being part of it. How much more moving is this flotsam, snatched from the tempest, than would have been the faultless and complete report offered by an organized film, for it remains true that this film is not made up only of what we see—its faults are equally witness to its authenticity. The missing documents are the negative imprints of the expedition—its inscription chiselled deep.

It is equally true that there are many missing parts of the film *Annapurna,* by Marcel Ichac, especially those out of which the climax should have been built, namely the final ascent by Herzog, Lachemal, and Lionel Terray. But we know why they are missing. An avalanche snatched the camera from the hands of Herzog. It also dragged off his gloves. Thereafter we miss the scene of the three men as they depart from Camp Two, and plunge into the mist, and only pick up the story 36 hours later as they come out of the clouds, after being blinded twice and with their limbs frostbitten. The modern Orpheus of this ascent to a hell of ice could not preserve the camera's sight of it. But then begins the long Calvary of the descent, with Herzog and Lachemal strapped like mummies to the backs of their Sherpas. This time the camera is there like the veil of Veronica pressed to the face of human suffering. Undoubtedly the written account by Herzog is more detailed and more complete. Memory is the most faithful of films—the only one that can register at any height, and right up to the very moment of death. But who can fail to see the difference between memory and that objective image that gives it eternal substance?

PAINTING AND CINEMA

FILMS ABOUT paintings, at least those that use them to create something the structure of which is cinematic, meet with an identical objection from painters and art critics alike. Of such are the short films of Emmer; *Van Gogh* by Alain Resnais, R. Hessens, and Gaston Diehl; Pierre Kast's *Goya;* and *Guernica* by Resnais and Hessens. Their objection, and I myself have heard it from the very lips of an Inspector General of Drawing of the Department of Education, is that however you look at it the film is not true to the painting. Its dramatic and logical unity establishes relationships that are chronologically false and otherwise fictitious, between paintings often widely separated both in time and spirit. In *Guerrieri* Emmer actually goes so far as to include the works of different painters, a form of cheating hardly less reprehensible than the use by Kast of fragments of Goya's *Caprices* to bolster the editing of his *Misfortunes of War*. The same is true of Resnais when he juggles with the periods of Picasso's development.

Even should the film-maker wish to conform to the facts of art history, the instrument he uses would still be aesthetically at odds with them. As a film-maker he fragments what is by essence a synthesis while himself working towards a new synthesis never envisioned by the painter.

164

One might confine oneself here simply to asking what the justification for this is, were not a more serious problem involved. Not only is the film a betrayal of the painter, it is also a betrayal of the painting and for this reason: the viewer, believing that he is seeing the picture as painted, is actually looking at it through the instrumentality of an art form that profoundly changes its nature. This was true from the first of black and white. But even color offers no solution. No one color is ever faithfully reproduced; still less, therefore, is any combination of colors. On the other hand, the sequence of a film gives it a unity in time that is horizontal and, so to speak, geographical, whereas time in a painting, so far as the notion applies, develops geologically and in depth. Finally and above all—to use a more subtle argument that is never employed though it is the most important of all—space, as it applies to a painting, is radically destroyed by the screen. Just as footlights and scenery in the theater serve to mark the contrast between it and the real world so, by its surrounding frame, a painting is separated off not only from reality as such but, even more so, from the reality that is represented in it. Indeed it is a mistake to see a picture frame as having merely a decorative or rhetorical function. The fact that it emphasizes the compositional quality of the painting is of secondary importance. The essential role of the frame is, if not to create at least to emphasize the difference between the microcosm of the picture and the macrocosm of the natural world in which the painting has come to take its place. This explains the baroque complexity of the traditional frame whose job it is to establish something that cannot be geometrically established—namely the discontinuity between the painting and the wall, that is to say between the painting and reality. Whence derives, as Ortega y Gasset has well stated, the prevalence everywhere of the gilded frame, because it is a material that gives the maximum of reflection, reflection being that quality of color, of light, having of itself no form, that is to say pure formless color.

In other words the frame of a painting encloses a space that is oriented so to speak in a different direction. In contrast to natural space, the space in which our active experience occurs and bordering its outer limits, it offers a space the orientation of which is inwards, a contemplative area opening solely onto the interior of the painting.

The outer edges of the screen are not, as the technical jargon would seem to imply, the frame of the film image. They are the edges of a piece of masking that shows only a portion of reality. The picture frame polarizes space inwards. On the contrary, what the screen shows us seems to be part of something prolonged indefinitely into the universe. A frame is centripetal, the screen centrifugal. Whence it follows that if we reverse the pictorial process and place the screen within the picture frame, that is if we show a section of a painting on a screen, the space of the painting loses its orientation and its limits and is presented to the imagination as without any boundaries. Without losing its other characteristics the painting thus takes on the spatial properties of cinema and becomes part of that "picturable" world that lies beyond it on all sides. It is on this illusion that Luciano Emmer based his fantastic aesthetic reconstructions, which have served as a starting point for the existing films of contemporary art, notably for Alain Resnais' *Van Gogh*. Here the director has treated the whole of the artist's output as one large painting over which the camera has wandered as freely as in any ordinary documentary. From the "Rue d'Arles" we climb in through the window of Van Gogh's house and go right up to the bed with the red eiderdown. Resnais has even risked a reverse shot of an old Dutch peasantwoman entering her house.

Obviously it is easy to pretend that films made this way do violence to the very nature and essence of painting and that it is better if Van Gogh has fewer admirers even if they fail to let on what exactly they admire about him. In short, the argument is that it is a strange method of cultural dissemination that is based on the destruction of its very object. This pessimistic outlook, however, does not bear close examination either on pedagogical or, still less, on aesthetic grounds.

Instead of complaining that the cinema cannot give us paintings as they really are, should we not rather marvel that we have at last found an open sesame for the masses to the treasures of the world of art? As a matter of fact there can be virtually no appreciation or aesthetic enjoyment of a painting without some form of prior initiation, without some form of pictorial education that allows the spectator to make that effort of abstraction as a result of which he can clearly distinguish between the mode of existence of the painted surface and of the world that surrounds him.

Up to the nineteenth century the erroneous doctrine that painting was simply a way of reproducing the world outside provided the uninstructed with an opportunity to believe themselves instructed and, thereafter, the dramatic episode and the moral tale multiplied the occasion.

We are well aware that this is no longer the case today, and it is this which seems to me the deciding factor in favor of the cinematographic efforts of Luciano Emmer, Henri Storck, Alain Resnais, Pierre Kast and others—namely that they have found a way to bring the work of art within the range of everyday seeing so that a man needs no more than a pair of eyes for the task. In other words no cultural background, no initiation is needed for instant enjoyment—and one might add, perforce, of a painting presented as a phenomenon in nature to the mind's eye by way of the structural form of the film. The painter should realize that this is in no sense a retreat from ideals, or a way of doing spiritual violence to his work, or a return to a realistic and anecdotal concept of painting. This new method of popularizing painting is not directed in any essential way against the subject matter and in no sense at all against the form. Let the painter paint as he wishes. The activity of the film-maker remains on the outside, realistic of course but—and this is the great discovery that should make every painter happy—a realism once removed, following upon the abstraction that is the painting. Thanks to the cinema and to the psychological properties of the screen, what is symbolic and abstract takes on the solid reality of a piece of ore. It should therefore be clear, from now on, that the cinema not only far from compromising or destroying the true nature of another art, is, on the contrary, in the process of saving it, of bringing it to general attention. More than with any other art, painter and public are far apart. Unless, therefore, we are going to cling to a kind of meaningless mandarinism, how can we fail to be delighted that painting will now become an open book to the masses and without the expense of creating a whole culture. If such economy shocks the cultural Malthusians let them reflect that it could also spare us an artistic revolution—that of "realism" which has its own special way of making painting available to the people.

What of the purely aesthetic objections? As distinct from the pedagogical aspect of the question, these derive clearly from a misunderstanding that demands from the film-maker something other than what he has in mind. Actually *Van Gogh* and *Goya* are not, or are not exclusively at least, a new rendering of the work of these two painters. Here the role of the cinema is not the subordinate and didactic one of photographs in an album or of a film projected as part of a lecture. These films are works in their own right. They are their own justification. They are not to be judged by comparing them to the paintings they make use of, rather by the anatomy or rather the histology of this newborn aesthetic creature, fruit of the union of painting and cinema. The objections I raised earlier are in reality a way of giving definition to the new laws following upon this mating. The role of cinema here is not that of a servant nor is it to betray the painting. Rather it is to provide it with a new form of existence. The film of a painting is an aesthetic symbiosis of screen and painting, as is the lichen of the algae and mushroom.

To be annoyed by this is as ridiculous as to condemn the opera on behalf of theater and music.

168

It is nevertheless true that this new form has about it something definitely of our time, and which the traditional comparison I have just made does not take into account. Films of paintings are not animation films. What is paradoxical about them is that they use an already completed work sufficient unto itself. But it is precisely because it substitutes for the painting a work one degree removed from it, proceeding from something already aesthetically formulated, that it throws a new light on the original. It is perhaps to the extent that the film *is* a complete work and as such, seems therefore to betray the painting most, that it renders it in reality the greater service.

I must prefer *Van Gogh* or *Guernica* to *Rubens* or to the film *From Renoir to Picasso* by d'Haesaerts which aims only at being instructive or critical. I say this not only because the freedom that Resnais has allowed himself preserves the ambiguity, the polyvalence characteristic of all truly creative works, but also and supremely because this creation is the best critic of the original. It is in pulling the work apart, in breaking up its component parts, in making an assault on its very essence that the film compels it to deliver up some of its hidden powers. Did we really know, before we saw Resnais' film, what Van Gogh looked like stripped of his yellows? It is of course a risky business and we see how dangerous from those films of Emmer which are less effective. The film-maker runs a risk, through artificial and mechanical dramatization, of giving us an anecdote instead of a painting. One must also take into account, however, that success depends on the talent of the director and on how deep is his understanding of the picture.

There is also a certain type of literary criticism which is likewise a re-creation—Baudelaire on Delacroix, Valéry on Baudelaire, Malraux on Greco. Let us not blame the cinema for human foibles and sins. Films about painting, once the prestige that comes from surprise and discovery has faded, will be worth precisely as much as the men who make them.

NOTES

SOURCES AND TRANSLATOR'S NOTES

THE ONTOLOGY OF THE PHOTOGRAPHIC IMAGE
From *Problèmes de la Peinture*, 1945

THE MYTH OF TOTAL CINEMA
From *Critique*, 1946

p. 17, Concours Lépine.
Annual exposition of inventions, at which awards are given to encourage French artisans and inventors. First organized in 1903 by an association of inventors and manufacturers, following an earlier exposition inaugurated by Louis Lépine.

p. 19, image on retina.
The notion of the retention of the image on the retina seems now to be discarded in favor of a new theory giving greater importance to the part played by the brain.

p. 20, P. Potoniée.
The dream of creating a living human being by means other than natural reproduction has been a preoccupation of man from time immemorial: hence such myths as Pygmalion and Galatea. Serious medieval natural philosophers such as Albertus Magnus (master to Aquinas) concerned themselves with the possibility. The creation of the homunculus is a recurrent theme in literature and has appeared in such films as *The Golem*. It was doubtless a kindred desire that

173

led early viewers of the film to exclaim, "It is life itself," such was the impact of the supreme form of *trompe-l'oeil*.

p. 20, Chevreul.
Chevreul, the subject of the interview, was a French chemist (1786–1889) who invented a theory of color from which the Impressionist painters drew inspiration.

EVOLUTION OF THE LANGUAGE OF CINEMA
A composite of three articles: the first written for a Venice Festival anniversary booklet, *Twenty Years of Film* (1952); the second "Editing and Its Evolution," *Age Nouveau,* No. 92, July, 1955; and the third in *Cahiers du Cinéma,* No. 7, 1950

THE VIRTUES AND LIMITATIONS OF MONTAGE
From *Cahiers du Cinéma,* 1953 and 1957

p. 43, Jean Tourane.
Director who made actors out of animals in stories in which they played human roles. He made two short films, *Saturnin le poète,* the hero of which was a duck, and *Le Lac aux fées,* featuring rabbits, a fox, a goat, and so on. He later made a feature film in the same style, *Une Fée pas comme les autres.*

IN DEFENSE OF MIXED CINEMA
From *Cinéma, un oeil ouvert sur le monde*

p. 65, Madame de La Fayette.
French woman of letters (1634–1693), author of *La Princesse de Cleves* and of *Memoires*—an interesting account of the French court.

THEATER AND CINEMA (*Part I*)
From *Esprit,* June, 1951.

p. 79, Boireau and Onésime.
The former is a character taken from a comic paper—a maladroit clown round whom a famous early serial was built. The latter was the central figure of an earlier comic serial.

p. 79, Jean Hytier.
A penetrating critic of contemporary French literature, author of a study of André Gide.

p. 81, Henri Gouhier.
A professor at the Sorbonne, well-known authority on the theater; author of *L'Essence du théâtre* and *Le Théâtre et l'existence*.

THEATER AND CINEMA (*Part II*)
From *Esprit*, July–August, 1951

p. 104, Christian Bérard.
A French painter (1902–1949) whom Louis Jouvet and Jean Cocteau persuaded, with some difficulty, to undertake designing theater sets. He designed sets for *La Voix humaine* (1930) and *La Machine infernal* (1934). He also created the sets for Cocteau's film *La Belle et la bête*. His illustrations of the works of Rimbaud are well known.

p. 114, Martenot waves.
"Name of a radio-electrical instrument which was an advance on the theremin. It is one of many electro-phonic instruments on which, at will, the player may make notes whose origin is to be traced to electro-magnetic vibrations ultimately converted into sound waves by some form of loudspeaker."—Groves' *Dictionary of Music*, Vol. 2.

p. 118, Jean Vilar.
Well-known French actor, formerly director of the Théâtre Nationale Populaire, which gives open-air performances in Provence in the summer, between regular seasons in Paris.

JOURNAL D'UN CURÉ DE CAMPAGNE AND THE STYLE OF ROBERT BRESSON
From *Cahiers du Cinéma*, No. 3, 1951

p. 126, line 9.
Does Bazin really mean "those happy few," sarcastically, or has his memory failed him when he actually meant "this band of brothers"?

p. 129, *Jacques le fataliste et son maître.*
A novel by Diderot (1713–1784), the Encyclopedist. The novel is in the line descending from Rabelais by way of Cervantes and Laurence Sterne, with acknowledged borrowings from the latter's *Tristram Shandy*.

p. 134, ". . . the deadly Nessus-mantle of the old Adam."
Here is a remarkable example of Bazin's capacity for compression.
In one adjectival phrase he combines pagan and Christian legend.
Nessus was the centaur who gave Deinira, wife of Heracles, a poisoned
garment with which she unwittingly caused the death of her husband,
thus avenging Nessus' own death at the hands of Heracles.

p. 134, "Kierkegaardian repetition."
A notion involved in Kierkegaardian religious existentialism. It involves finding what has been lost. It bears some comparison to the
Platonic view of the truth as "recollection," but is different as to the
temporal perspective involved. Recollection is oriented to the past,
repetition to the future.

p. 143, Viollet-le-Duc.
French architect and author (1814–1879) and restorer of ancient
churches and buildings, such as Notre Dame and La Sainte Chapelle.
His doctrine was that a building should be restored less according to
the condition in which it was found than according to the architec-
tonic principles from which its forms derived. The conclusions drawn
by him and his disciples were frequently criticized less for their own
sake than because their application would not allow for any alterna-
tives.

CHARLIE CHAPLIN
From *D.O.C.*, 1948

CINEMA AND EXPLORATION
A combination of two articles that appeared in *France-Observateur* in
April, 1953, and January, 1956.

p. 156, Salle Pleyel.
A well-known Paris concert-hall (named after the Austrian composer)
often used for the showing of travel films.

PAINTING AND CINEMA
Source unknown; not given in French edition

INDEX

181